His
Greatest
Hour

John I. Jacobs

His Greatest Hour

John I. Jacobs

PUBLISHED BY:
BRENTWOOD CHRISTIAN PRESS
4000 BEALLWOOD AVENUE
COLUMBUS, GEORGIA 31904

Dedication

This partly familiar but yet unusual book is dedicated to the countless youth and adult Messiah believers of any generation. They are always the ones who dare to search beneath the Scriptural surface to discover the deeper understanding of God's unbroken truth.

Those who dared to search deeply have been rewarded with continuous positive results which proved that no "one" Scripture contradicts the rest.

Foreword

The word "hour" must be noticed very carefully and properly associated. It does not literally refer to sixty minutes of time. It very simply denotes a certain period of time. It is used to initiate and fully accomplish that very particular activity. Any other explanation seems unnecessary for the interested reader.

This book contains a cohesive structure but also contains multiple segments. Each segment can truly stand alone. Nevertheless, there is a definite relationship or continuity existing among all the chapters. Comprehension depends on the reader's depth of insight and understanding. It would be an offense to the author to designate any "hour" as being exclusively out of normal sequence.

The author has attempted to maintain a non-creedal and non-denominational Scriptural presentation. He made no attempt to compete with, or use, any direct quotes from past or present theological scholars. He maintains his authorization on the basis of every Godly believer's available Helper (II Timothy 3:16, 17).

All Scripture references used throughout this book were taken from the New American Standard Bible. The author believes this translation to excel, in clarity, the present and past translations.

Contents

Introduction

Unknown to the community and world of his day, the child was thrust into history from his birth. Time was on his side from the moment of his conception. The Creator's plan for his life was launched ages before his parents' birth. His unique arrival and appearance in this world was not fully understood. It is easy to look back on any person's birth by normal indicators and happenings. These indicators make no allowances for unusual births. But what about them? We have no standard indicators to guide us because unusual births are very, very rare. It is most feeble, therefore, to say that the child's birth was only different. He was distinguished by a birth that was classified as miraculous! There was no other way to explain it! It was an unusual birth! It was a unique birth! It was a very, very singular birth! There would be no duplication of his birth throughout the existence of human history and eternity!

His first twelve years were considered to be like any normal child. He had not exhibited any "super" human attributes or characteristics. He was not physically a giant like Scriptural Goliath. Except for one brief family activity exposure, he was hidden from history. His personality and purpose were totally unknown to mankind until he reaches thirty years of age.

All of a sudden, like a shooting star in the night sky, his "humanly" beginning was revealed to humanity! It was so dynamic and unexpected that mankind was totally unprepared for his arrival! Who expects a comet to make a planned appearance? Who can adequately and correctly predict that arrival? Even those who were master searchers could not predict it. Are not all amazed when a new star bursts forth? It just thrusts itself out of the unknown blackness to prove its prior existence! Does mankind dread or welcome that appearance? Does mankind feel it is a hindrance to our understanding of this great universe?

The reader must see every "hour" as having no negative message or uncertain truth. If any "hour" does not show a totally positive message, then it will destroy the meaning of EVERY "hour." Thus, we would defeat the author's purpose. But worst of all, we would find portrayed a defeated life that lacked influence to lift humanity. Mankind needs more light to show new truths.

The reader now has a difficult journey to make. He or she must move carefully into and through each "hour" to gain the experience that is intended.

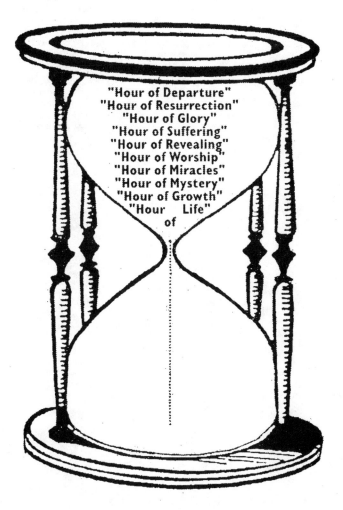

"Hour of Departure"
"Hour of Resurrection"
"Hour of Glory"
"Hour of Suffering"
"Hour of Revealing"
"Hour of Worship"
"Hour of Miracles"
"Hour of Mystery"
"Hour of Growth"
"Hour   Life"
  of

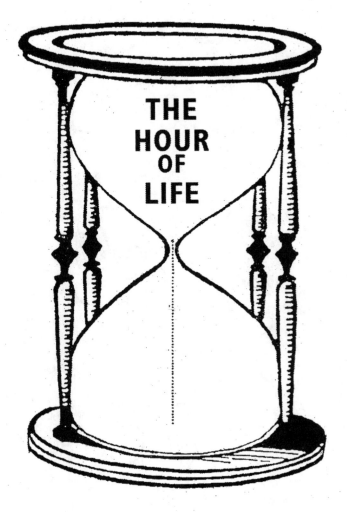

THE
HOUR
OF
LIFE

Chapter One

THE HOUR OF LIFE

Some cultures in that day had parental agreement for marriages. Those were contracted long before the female of the family was a teenager. We know nothing definite about Mary's situation. It became obvious that she had been engaged to a Jewish man who was several years older. An engagement was as serious as marriage. They each had vowed, by common consent, to keep oneself morally pure during their engagement. The penalty was very serious, in their culture, for anyone who broke that vow. Engagements never really lasted a long time. Mary knew that their marriage would take place very shortly. Therefore, she had been making the normal bride-to-be advanced preparations.

She had been so happy to hear about her cousin's providential blessing. Elizabeth had been so joyful when she became betrothed to Zacharias years ago. In a few months after their marriage, she had begun her hopes of becoming a mother. Her worst fear was realized when she discovered that their years together would be childless. She was unable to bear children! Her dreams and hopes were shattered! What had she done to offend her God? Would she ever hold a little one in her bosom? Her husband, who shared her sadness, continually prayed to their God. Surely He knew and understood their sadness!

> *"And an angel of the Lord appeared to him, standing to the right of the altar of incense. But the angel said to him, "Do not be afraid, Zacharias for your petition has been heard, and your wife Elizabeth will bear a son, and you will give him the name John" (Luke 1:11, 13).*

God had sent His angelic messenger, Gabriel, with good news! That was part of necessary events to present the Heavenly Father's Lamb!

Unknown to her, it had been six months since her cousin Elizabeth had become pregnant. She drifted off to sleep with happy thoughts about her coming marriage. She hadn't been asleep very long when it happened! She sensed a brightness in her darkened bedroom. What was causing that light? She slowly opened her eyes to look. Much to her amazement, there stood a man in shining garments! Her first reaction was to call out to someone else in the house. But before she had a chance to open her mouth, the man spoke to her.

She did not know his name nor did she ask him. She was sure she had never met him but yet he knew her name. She, of course, would never forget the words he had spoken to her. He had told her not to be afraid. But she became more troubled when he mentioned the word "Lord." He quickly told her that she had found favor with God. She knew it was no dream because her eyes were wide open! When he said the words "favor with God," she concluded he was no ordinary man. He had to be an angel from God. (His name was Gabriel.) As she waited with quickening heart, she knew he would soon reveal why he had appeared to her. According to their ancient Scriptures about God's contact with man, He used a most unique method. He always sent an angel, who appeared in a dream, a vision, or literally, with a personal, specific message directly to the intended person or persons. Of course, the angel always appeared as a male. The Lord had brought to her mind the Scripture account in Judges 13:1-25, concerning the birth of the man, Samson.

Soon, a wonderful peace came over her. She didn't feel afraid anymore. She sat calmly on her bed and listened to his words.

"And the angel said to her, "Do not be afraid, Mary; for you have found favor with God. And behold, you will conceive in your womb, and bear a son, and you shall name Him Jesus. He will be great, and will be called the Son of the Most High; and the Lord God will give Him the throne of His father David; and He will reign over the house of Jacob forever; and His kingdom will have no end" (Luke 1:30-33).

It took her a few moments to recover from the angel's initial appearance. But, as he continued to speak, his words caused her to wonder. She was puzzled and needed some answers. Had she the right to ask him a question? It was directly related to what he had spoken. Didn't he understand that she was not married yet? God surely would not want her to break her vow and His commandment. So, she asked the question. She must have a fuller understanding.

"And Mary said to the angel, "How can this be since I am a virgin?" (Luke 1:34).

Without a moment of hesitation he gave her the answer.

> *"The Holy Spirit will come upon you, and the power of the Most High will overshadow you; and for that reason the holy offspring shall be called the Son of God"* (Luke 1:35).

Mary hardly believed her ears upon the next words he had spoken to her. They were about her cousin.

> *"And behold, even your relative Elizabeth has also conceived a son in her old age; and she who was called barren is now in her sixth month"*
> *(Luke 1:36).*

What joy she felt when she heard about her cousin's blessing from God! Her cousin, who had been married a long time, was finally going to have a baby! But the angel said her cousin "has also" conceived. What did he mean? Was she, also, going to have a baby very soon after marriage? She had never heard of anyone having a baby in old age. Maybe she heard him wrong. But it was as though he had expected her to question what he said. Therefore, he spoke these last few words to her.

> *"For nothing will be impossible with God"*
> *(Luke 1:37).*

When she saw that the angel stopped speaking, she felt compelled to speak.

> *"And Mary said, "Behold, the bondslave of the Lord: be it done to me according to your word."*
> *And the angel departed from her"* (Luke 1:38).

As she had pondered the angelic confrontation of that epochal night, the answers, with understanding, had come to her. She did not sleep too soundly the rest of that night. She was humanly amazed by the night's experience. Not only the angelic appearance! Not only the marvelous words he had spoken! Not only the time of night he appeared! But

16

mainly, the full meaning of his coming! Had everything he spoke been the truth? He had told her of past events and future happenings. God would never send His messengers with nothing less than truth! The unquestionable truth! God had especially selected her to bear a son! Her son's name would be Jesus! That's exactly what the angel told her! She recalled to mind what the Scriptures said concerning the prophet called Isaiah.

"Therefore the Lord Himself will give you a sign:
Behold, a virgin will be with child and bear a son,
and she will call His name Immanuel"
(Isaiah 7:14).

She was that virgin! God was using her to help fulfill that prophecy from Isaiah!

She knew the first thing she had to do. She would go to see her cousin. Elizabeth would understand after she heard the story. After all, the angel had told her that Elizabeth was already six months pregnant. They had a lot to talk about. She had set out on the journey to see her cousin. She had decided to stay about three months. She had proof that something had happened within her that night the angel had visited her. As she arrived at her cousin's house, they hugged each other. Her cousin was surprised when the baby in her womb reacted.

"And it came about that when Elizabeth heard
Mary's greeting, the baby leaped in her womb; and
Elizabeth was filled with the Holy Spirit"
(Luke 1:41).

Mary stayed for about three months and then decided to return home. During the time of her visit, her own baby had grown in the womb. She was already three months pregnant! But wait! She wasn't married yet! What would people think about her condition? Would Joseph, her husband-to-be, think she had broken her vow? Nothing like this had ever happened to anyone before! She could not hide her pregnancy. She had to tell him right away and hope he understood. She was still morally pure. She had not broken her vow to God or Joseph. She would still trust God for her future!

The next morning, after arriving home, she sent for her husband-to-be. He saw her obvious pregnancy. She tried to explain what the angel had told her. Joseph had the normal human reaction. He made preparation to quietly and secretly terminate their engagement. He did not believe that her pregnancy was strictly God's doing. If he abandoned her now, she would be the object of ridicule and shame. It looked as though her future was filled with sadness!

"And Joseph her husband, being a righteous man, and not wanting to disgrace her, desired to put her away secretly" (Matthew 1:19).

Unknown to Joseph, God's plan for His Son cannot be obstructed. Before Joseph had a chance to work his plan, he was persuaded to stop. How? By whom? He was asleep one night and had a most unusual dream. It was so vivid that it totally changed his plan and life! That dream was the answer to the couples' alleged difficulty. It would force Joseph to reconsider what Mary had shared with him.

"But when he had considered this, behold, an angel of the Lord appeared to him in a dream, saying, "Joseph, son of David, do not be afraid to take Mary as your wife; for that which has been conceive in her is of the Holy Spirit. And she will bear a Son; and you shall call His name Jesus, for it is He who will save His people from their sins" (Matthew 1:20-21).

Now it was all clear to Joseph. He must obey the angel of the Lord. He quickly realized that May had told him the truth. His wife would be the blessed one among all the women of the Jews. Who was he to question what God had done? He would take Mary as his wife. He would not be ashamed of her! She had done nothing wrong. She had not broken their vows! His life would also share his wife's blessing. He would keep her pure until after the child's birth. God would require that of him. After all, she would give birth to the Jews' future Savior! He was so glad God kept him from acting hastily. He was thankful to God for not allowing him to be ruled by his feeble and unhealthy imagination.

Joseph quickly made his way to Mary's home. He told her all about his wonderful dream. His dream, in which the angel appeared to him, proved to him that her words were truthful. He asked her to forgive his doubts concerning her dream. He made the suggestion that they have the marriage ceremony as soon as possible. Mary was so overjoyed and relieved! She heartily agreed with him and the marriage took place as planned!

Shortly after their marriage, according to the time that was necessary, she journeyed again to her cousin's home. Mary wanted to see Elizabeth's newly born baby son. She had to go early before she became too pregnant to travel. She had remembered all that Elizabeth had told about her angelic messenger's visit. After all, Elizabeth's son and her son would be related. There would only be about six months difference in their birth dates. God had been so good to her and Elizabeth! She had to praise Him daily for His miraculous blessing to her.

"Now all this took place that what was spoken by the Lord through the prophet might be fulfilled, saying, "BEHOLD, THE VIRGIN SHALL BE WITH CHILD, AND SHALL BEAR A SON, AND THEY SHALL CALL HIS NAME IMMANUEL,"

*which translated means, "GOD WITH US." And
Joseph arose from his sleep, and did as the angel
of the Lord commanded him, and took her as his
wife, and kept her a virgin until she gave birth to a
son; and he called His name Jesus"*
(Matthew 1:22-25).

Unlike a normal married couple, there had to be another change in their plans. This came in the form of a decree from the Roman emperor concerning a census of the whole empire. It was necessary for everyone to register.

*"And all were proceeding to register for the census, everyone to his own city. And Joseph also went
up from Galilee, from the city of Nazareth, to
Judea, to the city of David which is called
Bethlehem, because he was of the house and family of David, in order to register, along with Mary,
who was engaged to him, and was with child. And
it came about that while they were there, the days
were completed for her to give birth. And she gave
birth to her firstborn son; and she wrapped Him in
cloths and laid Him in a manger, because there
was no room for them in the inn" (Luke 2:4-7).*

This HOUR OF LIFE totally belongs to God. He was the One who made it possible. Is He not the One who is the Author of ALL LIFE? Mary could take no credit in, or for, the miraculous conception. She was just the vessel God chose, but not against her willingness. She was used to fulfill God's plan for the Jews and all mankind. Her willingness to obey God had made it possible for her only claim to a place in Scriptural history. She had no divine power before or after her son's birth. Even though she was God's chosen, willing vessel, to fulfill prophecy, He did not provide her with what her son possessed. She had no saving power for humanity! She neither possessed any before, or after, her son's birth.

Joseph was of the proper lineage to become the accepted husband for Mary. He was chosen as the earthly father to make sure that moral and legal purity would be maintained. Jesus was not born by the seed of earthly parents! Joseph had no claim to his son's divine greatness. He also was not granted any divine power, in spite of his role, in God's plan.

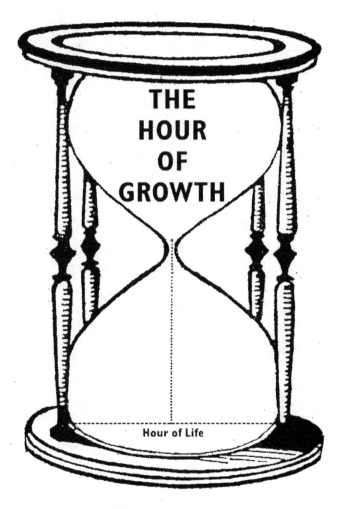

THE
HOUR
OF
GROWTH

Hour of Life

FIRST PHYSICAL GROWTH

Chapter Two

THE HOUR OF GROWTH

That baby boy had been born to them. His parents had thought they would stay in Bethlehem until he was several years old. But all of that changed before he was two years old. The problem was not their neighbors, or the community, but with the ruling king at the time of the boy's birth.

King Herod had heard about a prophesied ruler. He was to be ruler of the Jews. He didn't know when, but he had been told where. The King thought that any kind of ruler would be a real threat to him. Unknown only to God, the King decided to search for and kill the Jewish child. Fortunately for the small child, God had His plans for His Child! His plans had to be fulfilled. Nothing or anyone could have interrupted what God had planned.

Since Joseph didn't know about the King's evil plan, God took charge of the situation. He had sent an angel, who had appeared to Joseph in a dream, to provide warning.

*"And he arose and took the Child and His mother
by night, and departed for Egypt; and was there
until the death of Herod, that what was spoken by
the Lord through the prophet might be fulfilled,
saying, "OUT OF EGYPT DID I CALL MY SON"
(Matthew 2:14-15).*

King Herod became very angry when he didn't find the
Jewish Child. He heard that the Child had escaped. He
became so enraged that he ordered a great human slaughter.
Many homes and families suffered great pain and sorrow.
The king's soldiers quickly obeyed his terrible order. They
proceeded to locate and kill certain male children – all those
who were two years old or younger. No child was overlooked or spared. This was done not only in Bethlehem, but
in all the small villages close to it. He was determined to get
the right child.

Joseph and Mary had lived in Egypt with the Child as
long as necessary. It had been many, many months since
they had left Bethlehem. Since the Lord had sent them to
Egypt, they had to wait for His further instructions. Their
directions and command came in a dream again to Joseph.

*"But when Herod was dead, behold, an angel of
the Lord appeared in a dream to Joseph in Egypt,
saying, 'Arise and take the Child and His mother,
and go into the land of Israel; for those who
sought the Child's life are dead.' And he arose and
took the Child and His mother, and came into the
land of Israel" (Matthew 2:19-21).*

They then returned and made their home in the city of
Nazareth. This had been where Mary and Joseph lived when
they were married.

They had settled in the parents' familiar surroundings.
The Child had been born to parents who loved Him and

wanted Him. They had felt the need to establish some roots. Joseph was kept busy building a better carpenter's business. Many people had already known of his trade. He was a carpenter before he and Mary had been betrothed. He had not been forgotten during their temporary absence from Nazareth. He easily re-established his trade and made efforts to expand. After all, he had a Son to support. A father needed to properly provide for all his family's basics.

In the meantime, their Child named Jesus, was growing and learning. He was not only developing in earthly things but also in spiritual knowledge.

"And the Child continued to grow and become strong, increasing in wisdom; and the Grace of God was upon Him" (Luke 2:40).

It was perfectly normal that He became attracted to the carpenter shop. It thrilled Joseph, on that first day, when his Son wandered into his shop. That day became a habit as He grew older. He seemed to learn something new every day. His young mind wanted to know everything. As the questions arose and were asked each day, Joseph was ready with the helpful answers. His Son soon learned the first few steps to fashion a wood item. No man could have had a better apprentice at his side. His Son had shared the dream of every father in a trade.

Not long after they returned from Egypt, another member was added to their family. Jesus had a baby brother! He was Mary and Joseph's first earthly child. Their nearest neighbors were happy for the parents. They hoped the parents had decided to stay in Nazareth and raise a family. The neighbors treated Jesus and His brother like normal children. Of course, Jesus continued daily to help in the carpenter shop. He learned so much about the names and uses of carpenter's tools. This encouraged Joseph as he watched his Son grow and learn. Joseph always experienced pride when Jesus completed, with his help, a small furniture item. Jesus was also growing in an understanding of common people.

The years passed and brought other children into their family. His father, being a carpenter, had to work long hours to provide for his family. Jesus was still very young when a decision was made by Joseph. It was necessary to add a couple more rooms to their home. Neither Jesus nor anyone knew how many more children would complete their family. Has not the matter of life always been credited and established with God?

Joseph and Jesus continued to work together in their carpenter shop. It wasn't long before He helped to save Joseph a lot of steps. Jesus loved to watch Joseph work. He knew the names of the various tools. He quickly supplied the tool that Joseph requested. He enjoyed the aroma of cut wood. He had a liking for cedar and oak when Joseph made furniture items. He was growing physically strong as He handled the tools and the rough wood. Mary came often to the carpenter shop, with motherly pride, to observe Joseph and Jesus working together. Joseph was, and had been, a good husband and father of her children.

Jesus learned an important truth at a very early age. He had been born into a religiously dedicated home. They had observed all the religious feasts since He was born, especially those that required the males in the family to attend.

"Three times a year all your males shall appear before the Lord your God in the place which He chooses, at the Feast of the Unleavened Bread and at the Feast of the Weeks and at the Feast of Booths, and they shall not appear before the Lord empty-handed. Every man shall give as he is able,

according to the blessing of the Lord your God
which He has given you" (Deuteronomy 16:16, 17).
Most of the Jewish feasts were occasions of rejoicing. Most of the feasts were only local assemblies for acts and purposes of sacred worship. The three for males were great national festivals for general assemblies of the people. Jesus learned very early some activities that involved His earthly parents.

Mary watched her first-born Son as He developed physically and spiritually. She knew that soon she had to choose that special day. It was needed for her Son's full understanding of His place in God's plan. After the third child was born, Jesus noticed something. His mother, for some reason unknown to Him, was showing Him favor. Why? He knew she loved each child as every mother should. He knew Mary kept busy caring for all their basic needs. He had to be patient and respectful. The right time would have to be provided by His mother. Since Jesus was the oldest son, a certain responsibility had been placed upon His shoulders.

He had a good father and son relationship with Joseph. He had looked forward to developing His carpentering skill with Joseph. His father enjoyed the challenge of creating a new item of furniture. Jesus had always watched Joseph's hands as they skillfully fashioned the wood. Those rough, calloused hands were strong from using the tools, yet he was so gentle when he held his little ones. Jesus knew that Joseph expected Him to develop into a skilled carpenter. His earthly father saw potential in Him. It had daily thrilled Joseph because Jesus had become a willing learner.

Jesus was always glad when spring came. He knew what His family had to do. He looked forward to that special Old Testament observance. It was recorded in the Torah for all Jews to observe. He had remembered the exact date for the Feast. It was part of the Laws God had them to observe. Of course, the observance was for every year. It was always on the same date.

"In the first month, on the fourteenth day of the month at twilight is the Lord's Passover. Then on the fifteenth day of the same month there is the Feast of Unleavened Bread to the Lord; for seven days you shall eat unleavened bread"
(Leviticus 23:5, 6).

There were several members already in their family. Jesus didn't know if they had also looked forward to Feast days. It was easy for Him to remember because the Passover Feast came after His birthday. He had already turned twelve and wanted some answers to religious questions. He knew why they, as Jews, had always observed the Passover Feast.

"Observe the month of Abib (April) and celebrate the Passover to the Lord your God, for in the month of Abib the Lord your God brought you out of Egypt by night" (Deuteronomy 16:1).

He wondered what He could learn at the Feast that year. At the age of twelve He had an opportunity to again discover something new. It seemed as though they had met some new Jewish friends every year. That was another good thing about the Feast days. His parents wanted His twelfth birthday to be special and memorable for Him.

"And His parents used to go up to Jerusalem every year at the Feast of the Passover. And when He became twelve, they went up there according to the custom of the Feast" (Luke 2:41, 42).

Jesus had been impressed every year that Joseph and Mary attended the Feast. He had truly learned the great importance of its observance. He had heard it read from the Torah every year. He knew it was first recorded in the Book of Exodus, chapter 12. Their neighbors had no idea His family was more than just religious. Only Jesus' parents knew He was God's Son. The word about His miraculous birth had to stay hidden for a time.

Mary and Joseph knew that God had the time selected to reveal Himself to His Son. Had not the people of Bethlehem concluded that He was killed with the others? Nobody knew that God had protected His Son. Had not Mary and Joseph considered another danger to their Son? Maybe another king would attempt a similar action. Nobody had known the extent of evil that had existed in Herod's day. His parents had retained that well kept secret for His and their safety. The stay in Egypt and this new place to live had eased their fears. Mary had placed her Son in God's hands.

They had attended the Feast and everyone had a most enjoyable time! Jewish people had an unusual practice they all used in their praise to the Almighty God! Alas, all good, enjoyable times had to end. The time came for everyone to return home. The seven days required for the Feast were over. It was at that particular time something unforeseen happened! It was so unique that the Scriptures recorded the event!

Jesus' family, with some others, had started for home. Unknown to His family, He had decided to stay behind in Jerusalem. As the caravan of families traveled a day's journey, someone noticed His absence. His parents frantically looked everywhere. All their relatives and friends had been contacted. Nobody had seen Him since they left. Nobody knew where He was. After a thorough search, they decided to return to Jerusalem. Mary especially was concerned about her twelve year old Son. Who knew what thoughts went through that mother's mind?

It was a long day for everyone as they journeyed back to Jerusalem. That was the second day since the Feast had ended. On the third day of their anxious search, they finally found Jesus. It was only after someone suggested that they look in the temple. Mary and Joseph agreed, even though they didn't see why He would be there. Much to their dismay, they saw Him! They couldn't believe their eyes! What prompted their twelve year old to go to the temple? What reason would He have to be there? His parents became astonished when they listened! He was sitting in the middle of the teachers who were there. He was asking them questions and listening to their answers. Then He would proceed to ask them some more questions.

"And all who heard Him were amazed at His understanding and His answers. And when they saw Him, they were astonished; and His mother said to Him, 'Son, why have You treated us this way? Behold, your father and I have been anxiously looking for You" (Luke 2:47, 48).

Mary and Joseph had forgotten that their Son had a divine birth. Mary saw Him as only a twelve year old Child. She had not seen the growth that had taken place in Him. Mary and Joseph didn't understand. Nobody had known except His Heavenly Father. But, at that event, it was revealed. Jesus, God's Son, had an unusual spiritual perception that had been activated.

They had seen Him develop physically. They had watched as He acquired carpenter's learning. They had just been confronted with an outstanding statement. Their twelve year old made response to His mother's question and statement. His reply had to change their whole concept about His future.

"And He said to them, 'Why is it that you were looking for Me? Did you not know that I had to be in My Father's house?' And they did not understand the statement which He had made to them" (Luke 2:49, 50).

His mother, who probably had been more worried than anyone, saw a transformation. He was not just a Child anymore! She knew that very soon she would deal with a teenager. He had grown so fast. Time had passed so quickly. She had failed to realize her temporary earthly relationship to Him. She had to admit that He had never been disrespectful. He had never been disobedient to either parent. Jesus had truly remained a real joy and blessing to them! She and Joseph had to discuss Jesus' remark after they returned to Nazareth. As a mother, she had not been prepared for His questions to them. She also wondered how her other children felt about His questions.

Jesus had not changed from being Mary and Joseph's earthly Son. They saw His Heavenly Father open His Son's natural desire for wisdom. But His Heavenly Father still expected His Son to continue in earthly parental obedience of God's Law. Eight days after His birth He was circumcised. That fulfilled the Covenant God had made with Abraham. Also, at His circumcision He was given the name Jesus. This was totally in keeping with the angel's literal instruction to Mary.

His "Hour of Growth," that began His earthly life, had come to a close. It was probably more physical than spiritual because of several factors. His immaturity hindered His ability to acknowledge any spiritual accountability. His child-likeness needed to be in normal human behavior. He was part of a normal earthly family with no place for superhuman attributes. There were two differences between His family and a regular earthly family. One, no other mother had been chosen to bear God's only Son. Two, it was very unusual for both parents to be contacted by God's angelic messenger! This was truly an extremely unusual, and outstanding family!

He was prepared to be propelled through the longest "Hour" of His earthly life. It was still of great importance but yet kept hidden from history. He was still God's Son! No matter that the world stood by helplessly to understand the reason!

THE
HOUR
OF
MYSTERY

Hour of Growth
Hour of Life

Thirty to Thirty-three
    His Known
    Messianic
    Mission
    Completed

Twelve to Thirty
    The
    Silent
    Years

Two to Twelve
    First
    Silent
    Years.

THE HIDDEN YEARS

Chapter Three

THE HOUR OF MYSTERY

The world does not know everything about everybody. Then again, the world does not know everything about anybody. There are segments of time about every person's life which are unknown or hidden. That is true whether one has been a beggar, rich man, or king. Time is a recognized factor that does not change or fluctuate. A king living in a palace or a criminal placed in a prison. Both must recognize their necessity to yield to time's demands. Time shows no favor to the defeated or those victorious. Mankind's claim on time must follow that singular and strict rule. Whatever was or is planned must abide by that rule. Whoever activates a plan must deal with the non-variable rule. Accomplishments, or a lack of them, do not affect time's progress.

We are aware that Jesus had passed His twelfth birthday. Shortly after that, a veil was drawn over His earthly life. It seemed to duplicate the first hidden years after their return from Egypt. We know, for sure, that He was a physically whole and normal person. He was morally and spiritually perfect. He also possessed divine characteristics. One factor must be remembered.

"And the Child continued to grow and become strong, increasing in wisdom; and the Grace of God was upon Him" (Luke 2:40).

That tells us much about the hidden years of His pre-twelve life and actions. That veil didn't change His life either. We must remember that He came through that first segment of hidden years. He was still that same Son of God. God had chosen to lift the veil so that we could glimpse His Son's temple experience. We must also remember that He was a Jew and maintained obedience to the Mosaic laws. Behind that veil of God's choosing, we are confronted with the facts that were most obvious. We have an introduction provided for us by one very important Scriptural statement. It told us volumes about those hidden years.

"And Jesus kept increasing in wisdom and stature, and in favor with God and men" (Luke 2:52).

His whole life was one great mystery from beginning to end. The very Heart of that great mystery focused upon one segment of time. It was a veil that stretched over eighteen years of His earthly life. It began shortly after He was twelve and then ended at age thirty. Was that one of the greatest unsolved mysteries? Since that was God's mystery, only He could direct in its solution.

Has anyone been able to count the grains of sand flowing through an hourglass? Do they not flow, even though unseen by the human eye? Do they not flow, regardless of events or conditions? Is it not true that their constant flow cannot be perceived by the ear? Who has taken time or made the effort to count those grains of sand? Yet, the hourglass continues to perform its function! Therefore, God's eternal time cannot be measured, checked, or gauged by human intelligence.

The word "mystery," as applied in the Scriptural references must be given a token consideration. This must be mentioned before approaching that suggested "Mystery Hour." The Greek word means: "What is known only to the initiated." A regular dictionary gives an understandable definition. For the word "mystery" it states: "Something unknown; something deliberately concealed or unexplained."

The Torah does not contain the word "mystery." It is only found in Judaic-Christian Scriptures. There you will find it used a mere twenty-seven times. It was used twenty times by a self-acclaimed Jew. That Jew was born in Tarsus of Cilicia and had a good Torah foundation. He had grown up in Jerusalem. He was not only a Pharisee but the son of a Pharisee.

"I am a Jew, born in Tarsus of Cilicia, but brought up in this city, educated under Gamaliel, strictly according to the law of our fathers, being zealous for God, just as you all are" (Acts 22:3).

That testimony from a learned and educated Jew cannot be overlooked. Why? Because Jesus was not only morally and spiritually perfect but was also a very strict Jew. A little later we will notice His own words spoken for our benefit. We will use His words to penetrate the eighteen year veil of those hidden years.

The Torah, the Bible, or both are found with significant mysteries. They were recognized by the Israelites and other people groups. Those "mysteries" involved dreams, prophecy, and events. They were only to be solved by God's obedient servants.

During those early "mystery" years He was a very respectful and obedient Child. We could not have expected the Son of God to be otherwise. He had also been learning the basics of the carpenter trade with Joseph. In the Book of Luke, we noticed the written account provided for us.

"And He went down with them, and came to Nazareth; and He continued in subjection to them; and His mother treasured all these things in her heart" (Luke 2:51).

What did we just read? "He continued in subjection to them." That was not after He was twelve only, but long before He was twelve. We must draw the proper conclusion concerning what the word "subjection" infers. We must quickly conclude that He was never a difficult or problem Child. Subjection here means "to set in array under." The perfect Son of God could have never been disorderly or disruptive to family harmony.

There was one event that must have been a beginning of His hidden years. That was His Bar Mitzvah. No Jewish family would have kept their son from that important ritual. It was of great religious significance for any son. This happened when a Jewish boy reached his thirteenth birthday. Since we know He was already twelve, the veil hides His thirteenth birthday. Of course, we don't know the date of His birthday. Nobody has the record of the month, week, day, or hour of His birth!

The only way to see behind the veil is through God's holy word. The Scriptures do not mention Jesus' Bar Mitzvah. But neither do they mention His month, week, day or hour of birth. But we do know that He was born! The Scriptures give us unquestionable truth! That truth was verified and certified by messengers direct from God! No truth could have been more sure or exact! Since Jesus was born a

Jew, He was obligated to keep the Torah and its written Laws. That involved the five books of Moses. He did that and more during His brief lifetime.

Let's look at the idea of His Bar Mitzvah. All Jews were encouraged to read the Torah yearly from beginning to end. They also observed certain rituals for males and females. That was done according to the family's wishes. The son would have a Bar Mitzvah when he was thirteen. He would become a son of the Law. Whatever his birth date was, that part of the Torah was read for the ritual. The daughter would have a Bath Mitzvah when she was twelve, in the same manner as prescribed for the son. We must conclude that Mary and Joseph had wanted their Son to have His Bar Mitzvah. He had to first be recognized as the Son of the Law before He was recognized as the Son of God! Did not God sanction the Law first? Therefore, would not His Son have been associated with those who strictly obeyed the Law of God?

We have established that strong evidence in Jesus' favor. Proof of His Bar Mitzvah has set the stage for initiating that religious growth. His growth must continue behind that veil.

The search behind the veil is continued. When God drew the veil, did His Son cease to exist as both human and divine? After His Bar Mitzvah was He physically or spiritually idle?

Behind the veil, Joseph continued to have Jesus' help even after the temple experience. They were able to share religious matters with a better understanding than years before. It had been proven that a Jewish child's father was the source for his Scriptural education. That had involved part of the Shema, in that Torah section below. There was no doubt that the definite exhortation be obeyed.

41

"Hear, O Israel! The Lord is our God, the Lord is one! And you shall love the Lord your God with all your heart and with all your soul and with all your might. And these words, which I am commanding you today, shall be on your heart; and you shall teach them diligently to your sons and shall talk of them when you sit in your house and when you walk by the way and when you lie down and when you rise up" *(Deuteronomy 6:4-7).*

There is no doubt that Joseph was faithful and obedient to those commands. It not only applied to Jesus but also to Jesus' earthly brothers. We learned later that Joseph had been blessed with four more sons by Mary.

Would not Jesus have been more involved in the carpenter shop than the others? As the eldest son, He had a major family responsibility. Also, as a prior trained carpenter helper, His father would have depended more upon Him. We had no reason to doubt that Jesus' brothers also learned the carpenter trade.

Jesus' four earthly brothers were born during the veiled years, either the pre-twelve ones or during the pre-thirty ones. We noticed that He also had two earthly sisters born during the veiled years. All of these facts will have been surfaced and proven later.

During the pre-thirty veiled years, the carpenter's only divine Son shared in many normal human experiences. All of these were necessary for His total human development. God, His Heavenly Father, personally directed His Son's Spiritual development. All of these prepared Him for His unique life Mission. There is one thing of which we are SURE! No other God-Man like Him has ever walked this earth!

42

Some most important information must be included before we close this "hour." Whether veiled or a matter of record, God's only Son, Jesus, had a birth that is still a mystery to many millions. His birth began a process of fulfillment that had been prophesied about Him. His Mission for coming is still a mystery to many millions, even today. This veiled "hour" becomes clear when the other related hours are experienced.

THE
HOUR
OF
MIRACLES

Hour of Mystery
Hour of Growth
Hour of Life

THE WINE MIRACLE

Chapter Four

THE HOUR OF MIRACLES

He loved people. He liked to be around them. He also liked to see people happy. He desired to show everyone the way to true happiness. So it was no wonder we found Him in this place. No one could deny that this was a typical and happy social event, whether one was rich or poor. The celebration could have lasted a week or longer. That is, if one had observed the Jewish custom. And, of course, being a Jew by birth, he enjoyed the participation. Everyone enjoys a wedding celebration! It was always a happy time for the couple and their close friends. We have no record of the number of guests who attended. We are only concerned about one guest named Jesus. Why? Because no other person's presence held such great future importance!

The only person related to Jesus, at this wedding, was His mother. Of course, she was not mentioned by name.

"And on the third day there was a wedding in Cana of Galilee; and the mother of Jesus was there" (John 2:1).

Why was she invited? It is understood that she was there to aid in the feast preparations. This seems to have been so indicated as the feast continued. This whole account called attention to her fringe importance. Otherwise, how could she have known of the feast problem a little later?

He had grown to full manhood. No more a little boy of thirteen who had just passed His Bar Mitzvah. He was thirty years old and had already started on His life's work. As her first-born son, He was very dear to her. Is that not the way all mothers regard their first-born?

Her presence and alertness to conditions had fit perfectly into God's plan. She had felt she could share any problem with her son. Also, don't you believe she wanted to spare any embarrassment to the bride and groom? We don't know what sacrifice they made to prepare for that event. We had no information that their families were wealthy or influential.

Jesus and His disciples were among the guests who had been invited. No one had dreamed that it would become an epochal event! He had not wanted His disciples to be separated from Him for even one day. After all, they were involved with His special training and instruction program. Were they not invited because of their special association with Him? It seems unlikely that they would have been aware of the delicate feast problem that Mary had discovered.

Mary's discovery of the deficiency would have affected everyone at the celebration. In her mind, there was not a time or place for negative interruptions.

"And when the wine gave out, the mother of Jesus
said to Him, "They have no wine" (John 2:3).
We didn't really know what His mother expected Him to do. We cannot assume that she had any knowledge of His divine power. He had never performed a miracle from the

time of His birth. Besides, He was just another invited guest like His mother. At least, that's what the bride and groom had thought. We don't know the day of the feast that the problem arose. Since the wedding feast lasted only a few days, we must conclude that they were not rich. A lavish wedding celebration could extend into two weeks. Besides, what rich or important Jew would have invited Jesus to a wedding? At least, not before His confrontation with Nicodemus, a Jewish ruler.

The importance of Jesus at this wedding might be partly understood through three observations. First, He was the leader of disciples who recognized Him as a Rabbi, or Teacher.

> "And the two disciples heard him (John the Baptist) speak, and they followed Jesus. And Jesus turned, and beheld them following, and said to them, "What do you seek?" And they said to Him, "Rabbi (which translated means Teacher), where are You staying?" (John 1:37, 38).

Second, He was Mary's earthly son with whom she could share this temporary crisis. Third, this seems to have been a poor household. Therefore, Jesus, as a Rabbi, gave honor and distinction to the happy event.

We must come back to the crisis at the wedding. We realize that Jesus, as Mary's son, had to become personally involved. He couldn't ignore His mother's statement. He had respect for His mother. But was He one to have been so concerned about so trivial a matter? Mary, His mother, seemed to think so. What must her earthly son do? He had to choose the right course of action. Should He send one or more of His disciples for the remedy? How much wine would they need? His mother didn't really tell Him. Maybe He should send all six after the wine. This would have been more in keeping with what His mother expected. We know she did not expect Him to perform His first miracle! Her words to Him, very simply stated, were, "They have no wine."

We know her son was already thirty years old and the oldest child. Since He was the eldest, and according to their custom, He was the head of the family. That's why she told Him the problem. It is presumed that His father was dead. Why? Because he was not at the feast. She could not have expected Jesus to personally leave the feast. How would it have looked to the other guests? He had to observe proper social conduct and manners. She had to know what would have resulted if He had left the feast early.

An important guest's departure, a Rabbi, before the celebration finished, would bring dishonor to the occasion. Even if He had left just to secure some needed wine. The other guests would not have understood. What a big embarrassment both ways! After all, no important guest should have any knowledge of such an oversight. The honor of this home and occasion were at stake! If Jesus had chosen to leave, His disciples would have followed Him. They would not dare to question His reason for leaving. Wherever He went, they wanted to be with Him. How disturbing for seven guests to suddenly depart! It would have disrupted the happy atmosphere which must have existed.

Jesus was too thoughtful and considerate of His fellow man. He would never reveal the shortage nor leave the wedding celebration at that time. But something definitely had to be done. It was time to reply to His mother's statement. Did it surprise her when He spoke? He did not call her mother. She heard Him call her "woman." This seemed to imply reproof, as though the wine crisis was not her concern. But as an obedient son all His life, this was neither reproof nor disrespect.

"And Jesus said to her, "Woman, what do I have to do with you? My HOUR has not yet come"
(John 2:4).

Mary knew He meant no offense. She knew her son better than any earthly person's knowledge of Him. Her four word statement to her son was adequate. "They have no wine." She made no attempt on her own to initiate any action. No other persons at the celebration were aware of any immediate problem. The waiters were too busy doing their jobs to notice anything. Even the headwaiter was totally unaware of a shortage. What had been wrong with him? Had the shortage been purposely kept hidden from him? Had he not been responsible for everything to run smoothly? Notice the importance assigned to Mary at the feast. She hoped, as a mother, that her son had the solution. Those words had been guardedly spoken.

"His mother said to the servants, "Whatever He says to you, do it" (John 2:5).

Mary did not assign blame to anyone. She could have called loudly to the headwaiter about the crisis. But what would that have accomplished? Had not her first concerns been for the bride and groom? How would she have felt if something like that had happened at her marriage feast?

Remember Jesus' words to His mother? "My hour has not yet come." He was in control of His own destiny without any counsel from anyone on earth. His Hour or moment for action rested absolutely within His power. This same self-determination was noticed throughout His life's purpose. His mother had failed to see or understand the "personal" crisis He had faced. My Hour could have also meant "My time." The proper time for Him to intervene had come. Here, He had obviously meant, the Hour for publicly showing His Messiahship role. It had meant His time to decide His course of action!

His mother had placed the crisis in His hands and continued her primary responsibilities. This seems to have been the normal conclusion after the statement about "My Hour." We wonder why His mother had come to Him. Could Mary have been a relative of the groom's family? Or, maybe she had been a very close friend. We knew there had to exist someone with general oversight for this type of occasion. Her motherly concern for details seemed, and was, most obvious. She even gave orders to the servants as part of her role. They had been instructed to expect further orders from her son. Of course, we repeat, she had no idea what He had in mind.

Mary had a double relationship to her "grown" son. In the family circle He had been her son and gave her proper parental respect. In His life Mission, she was just another Kingdom servant, and He was her superior. She had felt every right, as His earthly mother, to have made a request of Him. In His unfolding and challenging Mission, she had to let Him decide. Had she forgotten the words He had spoken when He was a boy or twelve? "Did you not know that I had to be in my Father's affairs?" She had not understood it then and, at that time, she seemed uncertain.

He resolvedly faced the inevitable "Hour of Miracles." This "Hour" would pervade His life Mission. Up to the marriage celebration, His "divinity" had been kept hidden. It had not been for fear of man but because of God's divine purpose. His divinity was being exposed as His Mission was initiated. It would have been unwise for anyone to have regarded this as a forced or unrelated miracle. He had chosen to partially reveal His divine power and authority. This had begun the indelible impression which His earthly life made upon mankind. It would have been impossible to imagine His life without it. No one could overlook the depth, timeliness, and natural drama of that human event! The time had come! He would not have worked a miracle until the wine supply was exhausted. As goes the saying, "Man's extremity is God's opportunity." His miracle had to be free from the possibility of human duplication. It would have been impossible to see Him in action and then doubt His supremacy.

What about that miracle worker? He was not that hermit type of individual. His life, and the actions He initiated, cannot suggest isolation from society. Could anyone have imagined Him as a monk in a monastery? The first action of His Mission took place in happy and joyful surroundings. That had set Him apart from the self-righteous of His day. It took this social event to launch His identity. He appreciated and chose to associate with activities that generated true joy and hope! We are sure of one thing. He would not have been in the center of a drunken orgy! He would not have encouraged or persuaded people in a questionable activity! His presence always encouraged that real inner peace and joy!

Why talk about that first miracle? People today may already know Him as God's Miracle of Grace to mankind. Of course, He is that and more. Wasn't a wedding the proper place for God's love to perform a miracle? And all of that took place in the midst of normal people! It was obvious that Jesus loved being around people and sharing in their lives. We have never learned if the happy couple ever became aware of their crisis. I would hope that they didn't. Don't you?

That obvious miracle was directly related to the wine. It could have been called the "Wine Miracle." But we cannot overlook the significance in that event. It was needed for proper celebration in that day. It was connected with the fullest expression of shared happiness for the couple. We are persuaded that Jesus had a definite purpose in the miracle. He had taken no credit or applause for the result.

"And when the headwaiter tasted the water which had become wine, and did not know where it came from (but the servants who had drawn the water knew), the headwaiter called the bridegroom, and said to him, "Every man serves the good wine first, and when men have drunk freely, then that which is poorer; you have kept the good wine until now" (John 2:9, 10).

Here we have seen the proper credit given to the bridegroom. This was applied symbolically in Jesus' later ministry. The Scripture stated that Jesus' wine was the best. Why? Because He was and is God's best to mankind. He didn't mix the old with the new. He needed nothing from man to perform that or any miracle!

We learned some other truths related to the miracle. He was needed at the wedding feast to resolve a crisis. Is He not needed on the world scene of today? The world's answer for joy or happiness was and is not adequate or lasting. The world's "wine" has failed mankind. The "old" wine was quite limited and lacked quality. That quality has greatly decreased over the years. But, there is great hope for many! At Jesus' coming "Wedding Feast," there will be "new" and unlimited spiritual wine of superior quality. All who truly believed Him will understand.

"These things have I spoken to you, that My joy may be in you, and that your joy may be made full" (John 15:11).

They would be as filled with joy as the guests of the earthly bridegroom were.

There was no doubt that the word was widespread quickly about that miracle. The "new" wine was good news to Mary and the head steward. There seemed to be an abundant supply for the occasion. Well, didn't Jesus intend to completely solve the crisis? His whole Mission was to completely solve any or all crises. Fortunately, one cannot say He made a great show about His miracle. He didn't remain after the feast for the bridegroom to congratulate His action. What Jesus did had far greater meaning and significance.

How little we know of the divine intentions! We cannot dare to count it a coincidence that Jesus had received an invitation to that wedding. Was this not the Creator's plan? Jesus had to enter the stream of humanity! He was to initiate the fulfilling of God's plan for mankind. That was His main purpose. That second person of the Godhead had to act independently and without man's interference. His whole life had been planned to be lived by providence not coincidence!

The Divine signal had been given to His Son! Jesus performs His first miracle! Only He knew every detail as part of the whole. Here the two divine relationships deal with that event. We saw the Messianic veil lifted for action.

Mary's son is no more. She has no more "mother's" control over Him. He had severed any human obedience. He was launched into doing His Father's will in His own time. The miracle was initiated in keeping with His life of obedience to God. He had obeyed His Father by providing the divine solution for the Messianic introduction. Neither His mother nor His six disciples are to be given primary consideration. (He later selected six more disciples to equal the twelve He wanted.) He was David's prophetic son and God's Messianic Son. He performed the miracle by using existing elements to produce that which was non-existent.

Through the act of obedience He received the first glory due the Eternal Father's Son! This spark of glory grew to greater brilliance as His Mission continued!

You have seen what this "Hour" had accomplished. The final moments are upon us. The whole episode will soon be finished. He received glory when people believed in Him. What better group to have given Him the first glory!

"This beginning of His signs Jesus did in Cana of Galilee, and manifested His glory, and His disciples believed in Him" (John 2:11).

That initial glory was due Him! The beginning of His miracles related directly to His receiving glory. Has He been worthy of our glory?

The "Hour" has finished. Christ has received control to totally decide the course of His life. He alone has determined when each "Hour" will be finished. But, in the very end, each "Hour" must have given glory to the Heavenly Father and to His Son!

You have been granted access to the beginning "Hours" of the Greatest Life that ever lived! Be prepared to live the others as His life unfolds.

THE
HOUR
OF
WORSHIP

Hour of Miracles
Hour of Mystery
Hour of Growth
Hour of Life

INTRODUCED TO WORSHIP

Chapter Five

THE HOUR OF WORSHIP

The Hour of Miracles has passed. We turn to observe what this next "hour" produced. We had no way to determine the time difference between those two events. We do know that "worship" was introduced in the same Gospel. To properly appreciate this hour, we need to notice its providential setting.

No doubt He had arisen early that morning. Those who would accompany Him were notified the previous evening. He had made special plans for the journey. They had not planned to take any provisions with them. He knew they would have reached their destination by midday. The sun had not yet appeared on the eastern horizon when they started. They would begin their journey with a physical freshness. That was always the result of a good and sound night's rest. The mild morning temperature had retained the night cooling agent. It was the best time of day to begin any journey. They all realized that as they started with hope and high spirits.

They talked among themselves as they journeyed those narrow paths. In many places the path became dustier and the hard ground was not comfortable. But those were men who were used to walking long distances. They had been chosen to follow their Teacher wherever He traveled. They never asked Him where they were going to a destination known only to Him.

They had not traveled too long before the morning sun began to ascend. The gradual change in temperature was noticed by those travelers. The early morning coolness, when they had started, was quickly disappearing. But those seasoned and experienced travelers continued their journey. The hours slowly passed as the sun rose higher in the sky. They began to definitely feel the heat of another warm day. It was then that they saw a city far ahead in the distance. We did not know how far they had traveled. Besides the distance they had traveled and the heat, they began to feel their need of adequate nourishment. There was no doubt that the pangs of hunger were being experienced. His disciples had received their instructions. We don't know exactly what He told them to do.

"For His disciples had gone away into the city to buy food" (John 4:8).

The Teacher had journeyed with His disciples to a city of Samaria. It had been a tiresome trip, and He seemed physically weary. He continued alone toward a well and stopped to rest.

"So He came to a city of Samaria, called Sychar, near the parcel of ground that Jacob gave to his son Joseph; and Jacob's well was there. Jesus, therefore, being wearied from His journey, was sitting thus by the well. It was about the sixth hour. There came a woman of Samaria to draw water. Jesus said to her, "Give Me a drink" (John 4:5-7).

60

The scene had opened before us with the two main characters. It was inevitable that a dialogue was considered necessary. But those two had never met before. Wasn't there some kind of protocol that existed for strangers? We found that Jesus had started the exchange of words. But the other person was a nameless woman. Besides, she was a Samaritan woman! A Jew was not supposed to speak to any Samaritan whether male or female. But Jesus was not bound by man's prejudices, dislikes, or hatred toward others. It was about noon when He sat down by the well.

He watched the woman as she approached the well. He saw that she came to draw water from the well. Why had she come in the heat of the day? He was sure that she saw Him. Before she had drawn any water He spoke to her. He said to her only four little words. "Give me a drink." His simple statement to her was both timely and appropriate for the occasion. After all, He was sitting by a well and He was thirsty. Had He not made a simple and very human request? She had no idea to whom she was speaking, but she knew He was a Jew. She appeared to have been more concerned about their two differences. The taboo existed between them. Her curiosity caused her to respond to His statement. If He were new in this area, she had to identify herself to Him. Maybe He didn't know she was different from the other women of Sychar. After all, she thought, He had no knowledge of her life in that city.

"The Samaritan woman therefore said to Him,
"How is it that you, being a Jew, ask me for a drink
since I am a Samaritan woman?" (For Jews have
no dealings with Samaritans)" (John 4:9).

All of a sudden, Jesus started speaking words concerning a strange kind of water.

"Jesus answered and said to her, "If you knew the gift of God, and who it is who says to you, 'Give me a drink,' you would have asked Him, and He would have given you living water" (John 4:10).

She didn't understand. So she proceeded to equate His request with the drawing of regular water.

"She said to Him, "Sir, You have nothing to draw with and the well is deep; where then do You get that living water?" (John 4:11).

Jesus had not yet replied to her question. She proceeded to mention the original well digger's importance in the matter.

"You are not greater than our father Jacob, are You, who gave us the well, and drank of it himself, and his sons, and his cattle?" (John 4:12).

The woman seemed to have forgotten Jesus' opening words to her. She still hadn't given Him a drink to ease His normal, human thirst. The Jew kept talking about the water He had to give. If He has water to give, why was He asking her for that well water? She noticed that He was not carrying a water dipper. She was talking about earthly water, and He was talking about Heavenly water. That was beyond her understanding!

This Jew, whose name she didn't know, made a simple comparison. Jacob's well water satisfied thirst only temporarily. He stated that whoever drank of the water He gave would have no more thirst. She then asked the Jew to give her His kind of water.

"The woman said to Him, "Sir, give me this water, so I will not be thirsty, nor come all the way here to draw" (John 4:15).

Her understanding of His water gift was to simply reduce her labor output. She had not achieved His level regarding that "living" water.

Finally, seeming to forget His human thirst, the Jew makes an unexpected request of her.

"He said to her, "Go, call your husband, and come here" (John 4:16).

For just a moment, His request caught her off guard. She had not told Him if she was single or married. She wondered why He had changed their conversation about water. Thinking He knew nothing about her, she simply answered very quickly.

"The woman answered and said, "I have no husband." Jesus said to her, "You have well said, 'I have no husband'; for you have had five husbands; and the one whom you now have is not your husband; this you have said truly" (John 4:17, 18).

His reply initiated the turning point in their conversation and in her life. She was suddenly confronted with very personal words from a total stranger. Her mind was racing to obtain mental balance! Her answer came with the only thought that entered her mind. It was just a short statement.

"The woman said to Him, "Sir, I perceive that You are a prophet" (John 4:19).

A general statement about anyone who knew the past or can predict the future. Yet she still didn't know who He was. Right away she began talking about religion.

This was the second time the woman chose to address the Jew with respect. According to her religious understanding, He had to be a prophet. Was not a prophet greater than any king? There was no doubt in her mind. Yes, He had to be a Jewish prophet. Didn't all prophets have communication with God? The only way He knew about her was by divine insight. God only revealed secrets to His true prophets. She wished she knew His name.

Here she was in the presence of a true prophet. She could have deceived an ordinary man but not Him. Why had He introduced the subject of her husbands? Wasn't that her very personal business? It was strange that He used no abusive tone with her. It didn't seem to have condemned her. She felt the power of His word searching her heart. She felt inwardly convicted of her supposedly secret sin. She ought to have known there are no secrets kept from God.

Surely this Jewish prophet was more concerned about discussing religious issues. She had to quickly direct Him away from her personal matters. She always found it uncomfortable to share problems with a stranger. Of course, He didn't say she was a sinner. No doubt, as a prophet, He knew what God's Law said about adultery. She tried to inwardly rebel against His discussing her personal life and problems. After all, what solution was available from the prophet to have changed her life?

She felt that it was time to change the subject. Since He was a Jew, she quickly introduced talk about worship.

"Our fathers worshipped in this mountain; and you people say that in Jerusalem is the place where men ought to worship" (John 4:20).

The Jew knew she felt uncomfortable and objected to any further personal issues. He was glad she introduced the subject of worship. He had wanted to eventually talk about it anyway. There was no doubt that He was the authority on the subject. He possessed that knowledge because He was the chosen Messiah and not because He was a Jew. Of course the woman hadn't known He was the Messiah. No one had told her.

How little she knew about that Jew! He was the Anointed One! Why was that seemingly unknown prophet standing before her? Surely He hadn't come to merely debate existing and minor issues of her time. Why had that Jew so easily allowed her to change the subject? If she had only known! He had really come to solve both a personal and national problem of His day.

Surely He knew one was unable to worship God without a sacrifice for sin. Any prophet had understood that fact. She had talked about the places that Samaritans and the Jews had worshipped. The Jew had to get her concentrated on the true object for both groups to worship. He addressed her personally and directed her attention toward the only One she had to worship.

"Jesus said to her, "Woman, believe Me, an hour is coming when neither in this mountain, nor in Jerusalem, shall you worship the Father"
(John 4:21).

When He said, "Woman, believe me," she was then prepared to concentrate on His words. She had no choice because of His statements about her husbands. Was she expected to renounce her adulterous relationships? She had to believe Him because what He stated was the truth. He first had to tell her about the national problem which existed. Was not that mountain her shrine for worship? All heathen gods dwelt in local or national shrines. And were they not believed to be "holy" to their worshippers?

What had she expected that Jew to say? Hadn't He gently but firmly revealed her idolatry? As she continued to listen, He tore down her "mountain" of idolatrous worship ideas. She intended to respect His position and words with her. Had He not treated her as a normal woman of her day? She heard the Jew as He made a strong comment.

"You worship that which you do not know; we worship that which we know; for salvation is from the Jews" (John 4:22).

Had He said that to emphasize a truth unknown to her? She still didn't understand. What God had their father Jacob claimed to have worshipped? She should have known that. He stated that worship at their mountain had to end. Neither would the Jews worship only at Jerusalem. Was He prepared to reveal a better "place" where all had to worship?

Jesus said the "place" for worship had been liberated. He was the emancipator for those enslaved with idolatrous shrine worship. No more would there exist a certain mountain, valley, or city! No more was one needed to bow before an inanimate or impersonal object for an altar! The "hour" had arrived to change all worship. She and all Jews had to accept that fact!

This "hour" of worship had introduced a new aspect of worship, which clearly defined the objective. The woman's worship mainly involved the mountain, customs, and traditions which confined her. All she knew were the externals of her religion. She had never "seen" God, so how had she acquired knowledge that He was still "up" there? She was like most of the Samaritans and Jews of her day. Didn't she worship in the same manner as had her father and mother? Following patterns of worship without question are religious obstacles. The Jews didn't believe that their God was omnipresent. Their concept of a localized God had not changed. In spite of their expert synagogue teaching, God still dwelt on Mt. Zion.

Jesus' declaration that "an hour is coming" seemed to indicate definite future action. Based upon God's eternal NOW, the worship Hour was revealed! He had introduced to mankind a new phase of God's Kingdom. He proposed to initiate a new procedure that didn't need Jewish or Samaritan mountains. They all knew that God created those same mountains but not for worship shrines. The fatherhood of God was not limited to local barriers or boundaries. He had to be available for worship at any time or anywhere.

She failed to realize an important basic truth. There existed no character or personality traits connected with her worship objects. Was her mountain different from the others in her area? Had it possessed some unusual or unique features from the others? Would God still have been available if her mountain were gone?

Jesus proceeded to tell her what was the true object for and of worship. Was true worship only mere ritual and repetition as the pagans practiced? Of course, the Jews always had the right object in the Torah. He knew that as a Jew and a prophet of God. The confrontation with the woman was the first emphasis to worship since His Mission began. Hadn't the Jews placed importance and emphasis on it? Was it not an outstanding factor in every Jew's life? Jesus had purposely intended to associate Himself with the nation of Jewish people.

"But an hour is coming, and now is, when the true worshippers shall worship the Father in spirit and truth; for such people the Father seeks to be His worshippers. God is Spirit; and those who worship Him must worship in spirit and truth" (John 4:24).

She had never met a Jew like Jesus. This had to be an unusual day for her. He didn't show hatred for her as did the other Jews. What made Him different from the others? He had started talking about worship and salvation being related to each other. She had heard about worship all her life. She had never heard the priests mention a salvation. Wasn't one only required to obey the Law and the Commandments? This salvation was something new to her. Her life had already gone wrong. What did she have to lose by hearing the Jew's explanation?

Jesus knew what was happening in her mind and heart. He didn't overlook the greatest need of her life. That was the need for Jesus' living water! But it was only available after she experienced salvation. Why continue to worship a god who knew nothing about salvation? In His Mission He had some priorities. At the very top was the matter of salvation. Hadn't He appeared to exclusively offer salvation to the Jews? She didn't need a God who hated her as did the Jews. That's not what she wanted or needed. Wasn't it time she listened very closely to that Jewish prophet? Jesus knew that the true God of salvation worked only through love and compassion.

The woman didn't know that the fulfillment of two prophecies had begun. The two prophets were Malachi and Isaiah. The Jews knew there had to be only "one" true place for all worship. She had heard about two places. Where is that new place located where one worshipped in spirit and truth? She would plainly hear that the other two places had to be omitted. God had substituted a person, instead, for those two places.

The woman remembered that He talked about a new type of worship that was introduced. That was God's doing, and Jesus had given it birth. He told her to notice the proper elements that accompanied true worship. The main ones are spirit and truth. One must readily admit that feeding a creature had produced growth. Maturity and strength are reached with the continued feeding of the Spirit and the Truth. That uniqueness had to be recognized only by true believers.

He didn't dare wait any longer to enlighten her. The divine "hour" had chimed on eternity's clock. That which was divinely ordained had to be divinely fulfilled! All creation had been waiting. What for? That "hour" where worship included the Good News from God. We have ceased being restricted by the temple or tabernacle activities. From that fulfillment, by God's "special" prophet, we found that the true God was nowhere in particular. But yet He was also to be found everywhere.

The Samaritan woman was greatly blessed by watching a divine command performance. She saw it sealed by the most outstanding person of history! She witnessed that revolutionary action that transformed religious worship for all ages. It was initiated that very day and hour.

"The woman said to Him, "I know that Messiah is coming (He who is called Christ); when that One comes, He will declare all things to us." Jesus said to her, "I who speak to you am He" (John 4:25, 26).
Jesus had spoken those words to her. They didn't come through that "hour" ahead of time or too late. We knew that God's Grace had established His hour as the "right" time for the woman. That Messiah, God's Son, had come and was the narrator who always spoke the Truth.

The Jewish prophet knew that all past religious experiences had been replaced. He had come to introduce the only approach acceptable to the true Father-God. Worship to Him involved nothing of the Old Covenant. He had discarded the using of goats, oxen, or sheep blood in worship. Those were all connected with the Old Covenant. The Old was finished, and the New Covenant in His Son had replaced it. No one was asked to mix the Old with the New. The purpose for the Old Covenant had been fulfilled. That New Covenant provided everything that was essential to worship Him. His Son had rejected anything of the Old as useless and unacceptable. Both the Jews and Samaritans would benefit from the New.

She was seeing salvation's Provider to all Samaritans · as He challenged her faith. She had been chosen as the first

Samaritan to have heard the Good News of God. Her immediate actions indicated that He was the Messiah.

"So the woman left her waterpot, and went into the city, and said to the men, "Come, see a man who told me all the things I have done; this is not the Christ, is it?" (John 4:28, 29).

She had only known a form of worship. She had never had a salvation experience. God's Son had provided the proper confrontation to change her life. Her awakened conscience had been readied to receive His answer. The "prophet" Jesus had verified the Truth for her and all who later believed His words. When He said that He was the Messiah, she had begun a unique, life changing experience. She knew something had happened in her heart and soul. She felt that she had become a new person. If she had only known about that kind of salvation years earlier. Her life would have been so different!

The woman showed proof that something had happened to change her life. She just had to tell others about her very recent experience. She went into the city to those who held her in contempt and despised her. We discovered the results that proved she was effective.

"And from that city many of the Samaritans believed in Him because of the word of the woman who testified, "He told me all the things that I have done" (John 4:39).

Many more Samaritans went to hear about her personal confrontation with the One she called the Christ. They were also affected by what they had heard.

"And many more believed because of His words; and they were saying to the woman, "It is no longer because of what you said that we believe, for we have heard for ourselves and know that this One is indeed the Savior of the world" (John 4:41, 42).

They asked His to stay with them. They were Samaritans only who had come. The Jews hadn't accepted Him as Messiah. He had stayed two days with those Samaritans. They received the same Good News that Jesus had told the woman.

May I refer again to His prophetic interpretation about worship? His words had released their past limitations for worship. No more coming to their mountain! No more bowing to their priests! No more following ritual and ceremony! No more wondering where God is when they worship! That inner quickening they received overwhelmed their being! They realized the old way gave no hope for answers from God.

Did not the Samaritans have the same Creator as the Jews had praised? Did they not have the same image and likeness of God as the Jews had? Didn't they both need the same One to worship? The Creator God provided His Spirit only to those in His image and likeness. We are reminded what Jesus said about the object of worship. He said to "worship the Father in spirit and truth." Later He spoke the expanded word of truth to a disciple.

"Jesus said to him, "I am the Way, and the Truth, and the Life; no one comes to the Father, but through Me" (John 14:6).

His coming had provided all the answers needed by Samaritans and Jews. They also apply today for all races of people.

We have witnessed the gradual unveiling of that "Hour" of Worship. It was destined to become a repeated experience for all believers in the One True Messiah!

THE
HOUR
OF
REVEALING

Hour of Worship
Hour of Miracles
Hour of.Mystery
Hour of Growth
Hour of Life

TEACHING GOOD NEWS

Chapter Six

THE HOUR OF REVEALING

For many years a certain phrase had been used by Foreign Missionaries. They described their deputation work as "Show and Tell." Our Savior's whole life was to "Show and Tell" the world about Himself. We have used the Gospel of John 7:4-8 and 16:25-29 as the springboard.

He began by showing His disciples that He could turn water into wine. The result of His "showing" His power had caused the disciples to believe. Yet He "told" no person who He was. Sometimes, after this, He chose to "show" only and sometimes just to "tell." Any kind of "divine revealing" involved both factors. Here He was only dealing with Jews. We had just finished a good example of "telling" with the Samaritan woman. Only because of what Jesus "told" her, had she believed He was the Christ.

He was not persuaded by His brothers to reveal His divine identity. They had an ulterior and selfish motive because of His different birth. We knew that the pre-determined time had not been changed. He did not reveal His identity at the feast just to please His brothers. They didn't know the Jews were seeking to kill Him.

"His brothers therefore said to Him, "Depart from here, and go into Judea, that Your disciples also may behold Your works which You are doing. For no one does anything in secret, when he himself seeks to be known publicly. If You do these things, show yourself to the world." For not even His brothers were believing in Him" (John 7:3-7).

This was their way to show their contempt for Him. Were they not only rejecting Him as their Savior?

Had His brothers maintained their attitude for many years? We don't know. Have we not heard of a similar Old Testament situation? No doubt you remembered Joseph and his brothers. It would have been easy for Jesus to relate to Joseph's situation. Had not His birth been very different from the other family members? No doubt they wanted Jesus to reveal Himself to benefit the family. It had always proved useless for anyone to attempt to rush God in His divine purposes. He cannot be persuaded or pressured by human desires or attitudes.

Jesus had already planned to attend the feast at Jerusalem. The temple there was a most logical place to "tell" the Jews any truth. Of course, many of the general disciples planned to attend also.

"But when His brothers had gone up to the feast, then He Himself also went up, not publicly, but as it were, in secret. But when it was now the midst of the feast Jesus went up into the temple, and began to teach" (John 7:10, 14).

His brothers had no intention of hearing His teachings. Since they didn't care about Him they intended to ignore

His teachings. All they wanted was undeserved recognition when He revealed His identity.

His earlier revealing had received a mixed response. Some believed and accepted Him. Many Jews and others claimed He was a troublemaker. Attending the feasts was like attending a carnival. That probably encouraged people to attend. One always had access to the latest gossip. There was always the news of the recent political, social, and religious developments. The feast, it had been proven, was the proper place to present something new. Wherever Jesus went to "tell" something, there were always people hungry to hear.

The words His brothers spoke to Him had been true. The "hour" was readied for Him to stop being secret about His identity. Was He not God's Messiah? Had not the Major Prophets told of His appearing? Since He alone had to fulfill their prophecies, the time had arrived! He had to be revealed to the Jews. Of course He had already opened the secret of His Messiahship. To whom? The Samaritan woman!

If only His brothers had known and supported Him! They could have encouraged others to have believed Him! How sad it always is when your own family doesn't support you. They, no doubt, had heard of His earlier miracles. Who had remembered the feeding of the 5,000? Had they forgotten what the people attempted to do?

"Jesus therefore perceiving that they were intending to come and take Him by force, to make Him king, withdrew again to the mountain by Himself alone" (John 6:15).

The decision was made that He had to reveal His real identity. He was more than just a Jew!

The feast had been about half finished before Jesus made His appearance. It was probably after the third day of the feast. His sudden arrival had caught them by surprise. His purpose was to not interrupt the beginning of the feast. He had not intended to cause a disturbance. The divine curtain had been lifted. This was the divinely appointed "hour." The feast lasted about eight days. It was always an event for rejoicing. They celebrated God's provision for them during their historic Exodus journey. They were reminded of God's guidance with the pillar of cloud by day and of fire by night. It was a time of praise and thanksgiving.

The eyes of all were focused on Him as He spoke. The Temple was the proper place to "tell" about God. Was that not the center of teaching and worship? He came, and hoped that their response showed acceptance of God's truth. Were not all Jews regular in their temple attendance? What about every year on the Day of Atonement, when they came to receive God's forgiveness? Here He was as their "pillar" of Hope to deliver them from their sins! He came as their atonement for any day of the year. God had made this provision through belief in His Messiah. Was it hard for them to believe in God's sure promise?

Here He was at the feast to clearly "tell" them about their God. When properly told or taught something, doesn't that reveal? His disciples had addressed Him as Rabbi. He had no degree from the rabbinical school. Yet He had more than just traditional teachings to share. His knowledge came direct from God. Was He not classed with the unlearned peasants of His day?

"The Jews therefore were marveling, saying, "How has this man become learned, having never become educated?" (John 7:15).

Without any hesitation He answered with these words of association with their God.

"Jesus therefore answered them, and said, "My teaching is not Mine, but His who sent me" (John 7:16).

Before this feast He had attempted to reveal the Father's hand in His work. They had only known God as an invisible Creator. They had not experienced Him as a personal Heavenly Father. The priests had not "told" the Jews about a personal Creator. They had not emphasized the prophetic truth of God's coming Messiah-Son! At one time, He had spoken these words:

"But He answered them, "My Father is working until now, and I Myself am working" (John 5:17).

The Son had to "tell" and "show" the continuous activity of "their" Creator. Their Creator God had ceased His creation activity according to His timetable. He had scheduled the initiation of His redemptive activity. It had involved the Law and Prophets to start. By using these and miracles, the Creator-Father had partially revealed Himself. Jesus was the last segment for fulfilling God's redemption activity. He had finally "revealed" God's "faith plan" for redemption.

There was no doubt that the Messiah was well qualified to personally reveal the divine plan. No other person, saint, or prophet was more devoted or dedicated for the task. Who else could have spoken with such authority? Who else could have had perfect knowledge of all things? Who else could have known the mind and heart of man? He had been born to personally reveal the God to the Jews. He had been given personal, divine approval not once but twice.

"And behold, a voice out of the heavens saying, "This is My beloved Son, in whom I am well pleased" (Matthew 3:17).

At a later time the Heavenly Father spoke again.

79

"Then a cloud formed, overshadowing them, and a voice came out of the cloud, "This is My beloved Son, listen to Him" (Mark 9:7).

When God had revealed such definite identification of His Son, who dared refuse Him?

Only a brainless person could have refused the Father's Co-Creator. All the arrangements had been carefully made. The special prophets were selected and properly briefed. They had believed and obeyed an invisible Creator-God! Those few with faith had believed the special prophetic words. All had been made ready. The unique and perfect divine personage was revealed. He then became the unique revealer of Truth. All believers had access to spiritual understanding. They had actually "seen by faith" the Creator! They had actually "heard by faith" the voice of the Creator! Through that divine revealing, their spiritual understanding had been opened. Their new faith journey had begun.

God had uniquely and timely revealed His association with His Son. That clear word from heaven's vault came as Jesus' work began. We don't know who else heard those words. If they had heard, had they understood? His disciples heard that voice at the Transfiguration. God did not speak just to anyone with an audible voice. He was always tuned to the frequency of anyone's heart. Any person, by faith, could open his channel to hear. His Son prepared for the Father's announcement. He was the invisible God speaking as our Creator and Savior.

His "hour" for secret identity had ended. His Father's desires had to be revealed. He had not been silent about anything that was required. He stood before the Jews to prove His desired time to reveal. He had called Himself the "Bread of Life."

> *"I am the bread of life. I am the living bread that came down out of heaven, if anyone eats of this bread, he shall live forever; and the bread also which I shall give for the life of the world is My flesh" (John 6:48, 51).*

Later He used terms like "door" and "shepherd" to denote His mission particulars. They realized He was unable to hide anything. Still later He called Himself the "light."

> *"Again therefore Jesus spoke to them, saying, "I am the light of the world; He who follows Me shall not walk in the darkness, but shall have the light of life" (John 8:12).*

Many failed to believe and chose to remain in their spiritual darkness.

There came a day when He chose to "show" His divinity. Otherwise, they would not have believed He had performed the miracle of the loaves. He fed over five thousand people with five loaves and two fish. They were not satisfied and desired other proof of His identity.

> *"They said therefore to Him, "What then do You do for a sign, that we may see and believe You? What work do You perform?" (John 6:30).*

He refused to perform miracles to tickle the multitude's fancy. He had not come for recognition as a magician. Was what He had already accomplished not enough for them? Wasn't the fact of His "personal" existence as Messiah already proof enough? At the miracle of the loaves there was a partial revealing. They saw Him only as a miracle working Prophet.

> *"When therefore the people saw the sign which He had performed they said, "This is of a truth the Prophet who is to come into the world" (John 6:14).*

The next day, their understanding ceased about His mission. Look what God had done through Moses! Look how long they had eaten manna from heaven! This miracle worker only had five loaves and two fish. That miracle wasn't so great. They hadn't needed anyone only to fill their stomachs. They intended to make Him their king. Then they had a sure guarantee to subdue the Romans and obtain freedom. At least that's what they thought.

"Jesus therefore perceiving that they were intending to come and take Him by force, to make Him king, withdrew again to the mountain by Himself alone" (John 6:15).

He had not come to be their or anybody's king! It showed that they needed greater signs from Him. What He had already done gained no willingness for their support.

He had told them what His Father had done through Moses. Was He not greater than Moses? Moses' bread was only for their stomachs. Jesus' bread was for their souls. He tried to "show" again His relationship to their Heavenly Father. Their basic need involved not only the stomach but the whole person. He gave them a long explanation of why and from whom He came. He again explained His primary purpose for existing.

"Jesus said to them, "I am the bread of life; he who comes to Me shall not hunger, and he who believes in Me shall never thirst. For I have come down from heaven, not to do My own will, but the will of Him who sent Me. For this is the will of My Father, that everyone who beholds the Son and believes in Him, may have eternal life; and I Myself will raise him up on the last day" (John 6:35, 38, 40).

This "hour of revealing" was not about physical or material issues. Jesus' total acts and Mission involved spiritual perception. All that He showed or told had to enhance or encourage that perception. Was He not there when Moses performed God's miracles? Was He not Moses' superior? Was He not everyone's superior, in heaven or on earth? He had a greater challenge than Moses faced. He had to persuade material minded people about spiritual belief. That was no easy matter for even God's Son. Of course He could not have forced them to accept Him!

What was the difference between Jesus' "bread" and Moses' "bread?" Had not both come from the same "source?" Neither one was of inferior quality. The primary difference had to be found in the duration.

"And the sons of Israel ate the manna forty years, until they came to an inhabited land; they ate the manna until they came to the border of the land of Canaan" (Exodus 16:35).

Had not God provided for them until their final destination? That was what He had intended when the manna started. Moses had no control over the duration of the manna. He did not know what God had planned.

We compared Moses and Jesus in the area of knowledge. Moses had known only what God revealed to him. Jesus had all knowledge and authority by virtue of His divine position. He was the Son of God! He was God's Messiah! Moses was not able to "personally" promise anything to the Jews. Jesus, on the other hand, was able to extend and complete God's promises to Israel.

"All things have been handed over to Me by My Father; and no one knows the Son, except the Father; nor does anyone know the Father, except the Son, and anyone to whom the Son wills to reveal Him" (Matthew 11:27).

He had "told" them about spiritual bread. He promised that His spiritual bread would sustain them. How long? For only forty more years? No! Whoever accepted His bread, by faith, had life forever. Who had or has the ability to measure forever?

The Jews were not able to understand His words because of unbelief. To have truth revealed to anyone that person had to hear. Their spiritual hearing had been impaired by personal unbelief. They had to believe His words as truth from His Father.

God had guaranteed His truth in and through His Son. In centuries prior to Jesus' coming, the Father had promised His word. His Son had been speaking that word.

"So shall My word be which goes forth from My mouth; It shall not return to Me empty, without accomplishing what I desire, and without succeeding in the matter for which I sent it" (Isaiah 55:11).

They had been able to have access to heavenly language. But it fell on deaf ears. It also fell on non-receptive hearts. God's Messiah was their only acceptable "revealer." His personal message fulfilled the above prophecy. God had not provided for another messenger other than Messiah.

His whole Messianic Mission involved the revealing process. It had begun when we found Him revealing creative power. We found that in the miracle of water turned to wine. That revealing was very selective and personal. It had included His mother. He had revealed the true aspects of worship in Samaria. He had revealed truth, with proverbs or parables, in teaching. His coming had completed all the prophecies. The quoting of proverbs was not adequate for His disciples. His "hour" was getting short. He knew how to clearly and fully show the disciples truth. The time had come for plain talk.

"His disciples said, "Lo, now You are speaking plainly, and are not using a figure of speech. Now we know that You know all things, and have no need for anyone to question You, by this we believe that You came from God" (John 16:29, 30).

Before He used plain speech, He was regarded as a mysterious teacher. From their first day with Him they had received teaching. As their understanding deepened their questions increased. By His spiritual revealing their spiritual perception increased. Does anyone ever really understand all of a teacher's words? We have to admit, though, He was an exceptional teacher. Through a new approach in revealing they acquired access to clearer teachings. He was God's last WAY to "show and tell." But God's hand maintained the same teaching equation.

"But the Helper, the Holy Spirit, whom the Father will send in My name, He will teach you all things, and bring to your remembrance all that I said to you" (John 14:26).

The disciples needed the Spirit when they faced the dark days. Not far in the days ahead, they faced problems and uncertainty. They faced days of disloyalty and spiritual weakness.

The other Jews, not His disciples, had been skeptical of His position. They had known the history of the Miraculous Exodus from Egypt. They had quickly forgotten His lovingkindness to them.

"And the Lord said to Moses, "How long will this people spurn Me? And how long will they not believe in Me, despite all the signs which I have performed in their midst?" (Numbers 14:11).

That had happened not long after 1445 B.C. Not even a generation of time had passed. Why had their memories been so

85

short? You might say because their God was invisible. But Jesus was not invisible. He came and revealed the Invisible God to the Jews. Had history now repeated itself?

"Jesus therefore said to him, "Unless you people see signs and wonders, you simply will not believe" (John 4:48).

In both eras of time, the result was the same. Their faithfulness to God depended on successive miracles and signs. The Jews' attitude had not changed over the centuries! Had the Father wanted their acceptance without doing signs and wonders? The reader knows the answer. YES!

This "Hour" provided all Jews another exposure to Moses' Mission. Had he not mainly been chosen to reveal God's liberation from slavery? Moses now had power as a common Jew to free his people. Had he not appeared in obedience to God's will? Why had they refused to believe Moses' God of miracles? That invisible God had revealed His awesome power against wrong. Had not God chosen Moses as His personal human witness? Moses was to reveal the Father as their Creator and Liberator. The Messiah came to reveal His pre-exodus existence with God.

"And the Father who sent me, He has borne witness of Me. You have neither heard His voice at any time, nor seen His form. And you do not have His word abiding in you, for you do not believe Him whom He sent. For if you believed Moses, you would believe Me; for he wrote of Me" (John 5:37, 38, 46).

What good had been Moses' witness? Had he not been their highest historical priority? But had not Moses been dead for many centuries? All they had available was an invisible God and a dead witness.

Had anyone believed, after He revealed truth, with only words? What about the many Samaritan people? He had just briefly stated He was the Messiah. He had performed no miracle for them. Why had they believed and the Jews had doubted? Had not God revealed Himself when real faith was exercised? Were miracles always performed to present or portray truth? No! A supernatural power can be deceptive to faithless people.

"For false Christs and false prophets will arise and will show great signs and wonders, so as to mislead, if possible, even the elect"
(Matthew 24:24).

His "Hour of Revealing" encouraged faith in a person not some power. The Samaritan woman's faith was awakened when she directly heard Jesus. The other Samaritans believed the same words He spoke after they accepted her witness.

The Jews had developed skepticism and unbelief over many generations. There were many still living in Moses' shadow. They had not been weaned from a "miracles only" faith. The Pharisee, Nicodemus, was a product of that thinking. We first found him using that idea with Jesus.

"Now there was a man of the Pharisees, named Nicodemus, a ruler of the Jews; this man came to Him by might, and said to Him, "Rabbi, we know that You have come from God as a teacher; for no one can do these signs that You do unless God is with Him" (John 3:1, 2).

The Jews had been unable to see Jesus as greater than Moses. Even though Jesus had performed miracles of healing, they continued to classify Jesus with Moses. Wasn't He just another human like Moses? In spite of what Moses said and performed, they had drifted from God. Jesus had revealed truths that outdated Moses' whole Mission. They were unable to see Jesus as a greater revealer of truth. They saw Moses as first in their history and Jesus as secondary in importance.

*"We know that God has spoken to Moses, but as
for this man, we do not know where He is from"
(John 9:29).*

The "Hour of Revealing" was rapidly growing shorter.
There was so much more His disciples needed to know. He
knew He couldn't tell them but a little at a time. He had
introduced His disciples to another Revealer. He was called
the Spirit of Truth. The "Door" of truth had been opened.
No man or king had power to close that door.

*"But I tell you the truth, it is to your advantage
that I go away; for if I do not go away, the Helper
shall not come to you; but if I go, I will send Him
to you" (John 16:7).*

The new Revealer possessed all the answers because He
knew all the questions. His Heavenly Father, through
prayer, made provision for acquiring necessary revelation.
Their faith and obedience was required. His Father guaranteed personal attention and unlimited access. There was no
restriction on the number of times He was asked.

*"But the Helper, the Holy Spirit, whom the Father
will send in my name, He will teach you all things,
and bring to your remembrance all that I said to
you" (John 14:26).*

The new Helper or Revealer had been promised to
walk with them. The disciples found the Messiah available for all their needs. God had always kept His promise
to every believer. That had never changed. That Spirit of
Truth, though invisible, was always accessible. He possessed the same power and authority as He revealed
Jesus' teachings.

*"But when He, the Spirit of Truth, comes, He will
guide you into all the truth; for He will not speak
on His own initiative, but whatever He hears, He*

will speak; and He will disclose to you what is to come" (John 16:13).

He possessed the divine insight to know all about mankind. Nothing was hidden from His knowledge! The past and present was an open book to Him. He also knew what any person's future contained!

Jesus had used parables in various situations of teaching. But there came a time when the disciples needed simplicity. He did not always confuse them with scholarly presentations. He dealt mainly with unskilled people of academic limitations. He did not come only to the rich and highly educated individuals. Jesus was able to speak with both earthly and heavenly language. Notice first what He had said to Nicodemus.

"If I told you earthly things and you do not believe, how shall you believe if I tell you of heavenly things" (John 3:12).

He had been speaking to an educated Pharisee. How different from most of His disciples! He knew there were no human words or expressions for some tasks. He had to present an acceptable and sufficient explanation of the Father. They had not understood earlier. He was God's divine communicator to the Jews. His earthly external presentations needed additional emphasis and clarifying.

"These things have I spoken to you in figurative language; an hour is coming when I will no more speak to you in figurative language, but will tell you openly of the Father" (John 16:25).

The moment had come to remove any veil of misunderstanding. There had to be unquestionable openness during the critical hour. He presented His last personal mention of His Mission Goal. He did so after carefully and frankly phrasing the words. He hadn't seemed completely

89

satisfied they had complete understanding. At a later day, after He left, the Holy Spirit brought full understanding. He finally introduced two important words to His disciples. These words are also applicable to all His followers. They are "prayer" and "love." These are timeless for divine-human communication.

> *"In that day you will ask in My name, and I do not say to you that I will request the Father on your behalf; for the Father Himself loves you, because you have loved Me, and have believed that I came forth from the Father" (John 16:26, 27).*

How much clearer could that have been to them? His Father provided assurance of prayer participation with believers. Again, we must say, God cannot negate His own word. Had not Jesus primarily come to reveal His Father's love? That had been no easy Mission! There existed no faith until God revealed His Love Messenger. Was that divine Messenger successful? Yes! But the Jews had not accepted His divine credentials! The Jews who refused Jesus' Love didn't love Moses either.

His disciples were very special. He was their Teacher who always revealed truth to them. His promises had been kept on the earth. They are continued into eternity. He revealed to them the deepest mysteries of the divine. They had believed in Him in spite of His miracles. How different they were from the other Jews. How different they were from the multitudes who needed signs and wonders!

There was no doubt of His oneness with the Father. He shared this truth as His Mission neared its end. Many unbelievers had rejected His revealed mysteries and signs. As the "Hour of Revealing" ended, He made a last statement. He addressed the yet immature disciples with an ominous revelation.

"Behold, an hour is coming, and has already come, for you to be scattered, each to his own home, and to leave me alone; and yet I am not alone, because the Father is with me" (John 16:32).

The "Hour of Revealing" ceased its flow. All He had revealed was accomplished. He knew what was ahead. The disciples had not understood His meaning. Creation seemed to shudder as the next "hour" was considered. There had to be no delay. Man's eternal destiny had hung in the balance!

Don't continue reading unless you have strong convictions about justice!

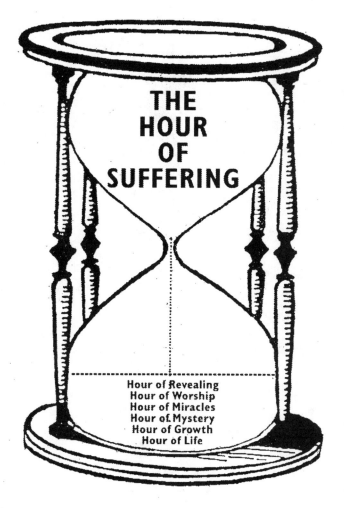

THE
HOUR
OF
SUFFERING

Hour of Revealing
Hour of Worship
Hour of Miracles
Hour of Mystery
Hour of Growth
Hour of Life

BEARING OUR CHASTENING

Chapter Seven

THE HOUR OF SUFFERING

He did not expect to enter a happy or cheerful "Hour." The atmosphere was totally charged with negative attitudes toward Messiah. It was filled with hatred, threats, and expectations of isolation. It was as though a contagious disease had stricken men's hearts. One must have wondered about this "hour." Did He have to face it? He had to fulfill that declared prophecy of Isaiah. No prophet had described it better than he.

"He was despised and forsaken of men, a man of sorrows, and acquainted with grief; and like one from whom men hide their face, He was despised, and we did not esteem Him" (Isaiah 53:3).

This beginning sounded terrible, but the unbelievable was just ahead!

Not many months ago, the Jews intended to arrange His arrest. Separation from friends and loved ones involves mental anguish. He knew their intentions were far beyond that.

They had several good opportunities to seize Him. The idea had germinated in their minds long before this action. They were impatient with the indecision of the Roman government. A person might have equated their actions to that of vigilantes. We must notice their attempts and the quick results. The multitude was a temporary delay for the Pharisees hatred.

"And when they sought to seize Him, they became afraid of the multitudes, because they held Him to be a prophet" (Matthew 21:46).

It was awful that Jewish leaders were His greatest opposers. That was a definite indictment against their ability to spread truth. The multitudes seemed to possess a better perception than their leaders. Their willingness to believe in Jesus gave them a clear focus on truth. We noticed their opened minds.

"But many of the multitude believed in Him; and they were saying, "When the Christ shall come, He will not perform more signs than those which this man has, will He?" (John 7:31).

The two religious parties, who normally were opposite, had agreed against Him. They had totally ignored the people's understanding. Why? The leaders saw Jesus as threatening their popularity and power.

Their only thought from the beginning was to kill Him. They had thought it to be simple and easy. After all, He was only one man against all of them. There were several who attempted to seize Jesus. They had to arrange the proper punishment afterward. Their spiritual insight was zero. This Messiah knew their intentions were evil. His Heavenly Father also knew their intentions.

"They were seeking therefore to seize Him; and no man laid his hand on Him, because His hour had not yet come" (John 7:30).

They are stopped by a mysterious and unusual force. How blinded and ignorant are they to their Creator's power!

The Messiah was still controlling His Mission under divine direction. He was not ready yet to face them. The religious leaders were ignorant of Jesus' power and authority. Hear the statement He made not long afterward.

"Or do you think that I cannot appeal to My Father, and He will at once put at my disposal more than twelve legions of angels?"
(Matthew 26:53).

They made other attempts to seize Him. Their attempt to incite the crowd against Him had failed. Their hope for victory had disappeared. Why had they failed? Was it not because of divine intention for His Son's Mission? What about God's timetable? No religious leader or king possessed power to change it!

There had to exist suffering anywhere that hatred was allowed to thrive. Of course, God never did sanction or encourage hatred. No matter how hatred planned to develop, it was inadequate to deter God's plan. We are sure that Satan provides the initiative for hatred to breed. God sets the boundaries for hatred's growth. No matter how high their waves or how strong their tides. Workers of hatred seem to delight in unnecessary pain and suffering.

The Messiah knew the Scribes and Pharisees hated Him. They had planned to seize Him as He taught. They knew whenever He came to the temple.

"And after these things Jesus was walking in Galilee; for He was unwilling to walk in Judea, because the Jews were seeking to kill Him"
(John 7:1).

Their hatred grew when He claimed divinity with the Father. Everything He taught about their Creator-God increased their animosity. They made an attempt to seize Him but were stopped. The reason was stated for us.

"These words He spoke in the treasury, as He taught in the temple; and no one seized Him, because His hour had not come" (John 8:20).

They again picked the wrong time. God did not tolerate their interference. Jesus' words here became the turning point in their plan. They believed that nothing or anyone could stop their devious plan. The religious leaders had acquired uncaring allies. Their support would suffice until He was seized and killed. They finally heard Him make an unbelievable claim. They now had the right reason to kill Him. His two statements were all they needed.

"Your father Abraham rejoiced to see My day, and he saw it and was glad." Jesus said to them, "Truly, truly, I say to you, before Abraham was born, I AM." Therefore they picked up stones to throw at Him; but Jesus hid Himself, and went out of the temple" (John 8:56, 58, 59).

He hid under the Father's protection and left the temple. Some believe a sympathetic crowd provided His escape. However it happened, we knew God was behind it!

The religious leaders didn't understand the prime importance of God's plan. They hoped to persuade the crowd to help them seize Him. But that had not been successful in the past. The crowd had seemed to like Him. They enjoyed watching Him perform miracles. They had to be careful. What if they had caused a negative attitude toward themselves? They needed the right occasion and time to get crowd support. The feast activity seemed the proper time.

The religious leaders had decided on His future because He threatened their authority. They planned to lie to the people about their protective efforts. We saw them enlarge that idea. The people would believe their lies. The feast hadn't ended yet. No doubt He planned to stay until the last day. That had to be the proper time to make the attempt. They had piled up many actions that helped their positions.

Had He not healed a man on their Sabbath? His miracle of healing had set a dangerous motive for people. They had to keep the people ignorant of the Law's real purpose. Go back to the beginning of the feast in Jerusalem. See the miracle performed and the Jews reaction.

> *"Jesus said to him, "Arise, take up your pallet, and walk." Therefore the Jews were saying to him who was cured, "It is the Sabbath, and it is not permissible for you to carry your pallet"*
> *(John 5:8, 10).*

They saw only the man's illegal pallet carrying and not the miracle. Was it possible the five thousand He fed got the wrong idea? The appointed officers didn't understand that there was a proper hour. To which hour are we referring? That "hour" of extreme agony and death! They knew that without His arrest there would be no false trial. The final hour had to wait for that successful arrest.

The last day of the Feast was upon them. The crowds started leaving for their homes. The long awaited opportunity had come. They had to act at the Feast of Booths. The arresting officers were sent out! They had been gone too long! It was past time for their return! They finally returned without Jesus. What had happened?

> *"The officers therefore came to the chief priests and Pharisees and they said to them, "Why did you not bring Him?" The officers answered, "Never did a man speak the way this man speaks." The Pharisees therefore answered them, "You have not also been led astray, have you?" (John 7:45-47).*

Like the Samaritan woman, they had also forgotten something! She forgot her water jug, and they had forgotten their mission. The Pharisees had called the multitudes accursed. Had not the arresting officers been blessed by the truth?

All events had to happen in God's design! We are powerless to hasten or slow down God's plan. The opposition to Jesus had basically begun in their hearts. Then began the gradual development into sheer hatred. He had done nothing outwardly to demean them. Their opposition continued to grow into rejection, hatred, and lastly, murder. Mankind had not changed that order since the beginning. They possessed no desire or ability to stop themselves. Like a boulder speeding unchecked down a mountainside. Blinded by unbelief, they were consumed with their evil intentions.

They had initially judged Jesus by their hypocritical religious position. That had hardened their persistent unbelieving hearts. They, as Moses had, were opposing God's plan of deliverance. God had succeeded with Moses. He had planned success with His Son. God, as Spirit, very easily delayed their evil actions. Only when the "divine clock" struck did God's Son enter His suffering. Not any sooner or any later.

Jesus had realized one truth evident from the last feast day. He knew His Jewish enemies were persuaded to seize Him. He proceeded to immediately inform them of a time factor. It seemed He knew His earthly life would end. His opposers had to hasten their plan. They were very "law" conscious. Everything had to be strictly legal. (We knew His Mission had to end in death.) His divine determination had already given Him victory. His enemies would be unable to pursue Him where He was going.

"Jesus therefore said, "For a little while longer I am with you, then I go to Him who sent Me. You

100

*shall seek Me, and shall not find Me, and where I
am, you cannot come" (John 7:33, 34).*

He had another important truth for the religious leaders. He had to tell them of His pre-existent state. Couldn't
they tell He was not of this world? They had to believe that
He and the Father were One. After that attempt to enlighten
their minds had failed, He tried another approach to open
their understanding.

*"They did not realize that He had been speaking to
them about the Father" (John 8:27).*

He knew they didn't really believe in the Father. They had
remembered Moses but had forgotten his God. When Jesus
claimed to be that same God, they were furious! They had
again rejected His words of truth. To them He was a blasphemer. They had to stop His words by any means available.
He had performed a miracle by healing a blind man. The
Jews rejected Jesus in their questions to the blind man.

*"And they reviled him and said, "You are His dis-
ciple, but we are disciples of Moses. We know that
God has spoken to Moses; but as for this man, we
do not know where He is from" (John 9:28, 29).*

They were fanatical in their persistence to stop Him.
Since the temple was unfinished, there were loose stones available. At the Feast of Dedication He faced the last attempt to
stone Him. He had just spoken that great eternal security for
believers. There is not a greater one in all the Bible.

*"My sheep hear My voice, and I know them, and
they follow Me; and I give eternal life to them, and
they shall never perish; and no one shall snatch
them out of my hand. My Father, who has given
them to Me, is greater than all; and no one is able
to snatch them out of the Father's hand. I and the
Father are one" (John 10:27-30).*

Notice the Jews immediate response to that great message.

"The Jews took up stones again to stone Him"
(John 10:31).

He had now faced extreme violence with all its ugliness. Their laws had stated that they could stone a blasphemer. They would be justified before the people. But maybe believers and disciples intended to help Him. What could they do? As fellow Jews, they also were aware of that same law. The religious leaders' hatred was prepared to erupt like a volcano. It had been smoldering for many months.

At an earlier time, He had appeared immune to their hatred. He had been protected by divine purpose. We knew "His hour had not yet come." He had experienced unlimited protection under God's perfect will. The episode at Solomon's portico seemed to have indicated uncertainty. It was hard to imagine His humanity in that episode. How would you and I have felt? He was confronted by a hostile and threatening crowd. Of course He had friends, but many more enemies. He tried to use a different approach. He introduced the idea, known to them, of doing good works. They had believed that was basic for all Jews. As they were about to throw the stones, He spoke.

"Jesus answered them, "I showed you many good
works from the Father; for which of them are you
stoning Me?" The Jews answered Him, "For a
good work we do not stone You, but for blasphemy,
and because You, being a man, made Yourself out
to be God" (John 10:32-33).

We saw the real problem come to the surface. They didn't believe that their God had sent Him. That was the reason they didn't accept the miracles. Of course, they realized as mere men, they also possessed no miracle power. They also had blinded their eyes and hardened their hearts.

Their faith in God was almost non-existent. They possessed great faith only in themselves. He made a last effort to open their reasoning.

"If I do not do the works of My Father, do not believe Me; but if I do them, though you do not believe Me, believe the works, that you may know and understand that the Father is in Me, and I in the Father" (John 10:37, 38).

The effort He made had again fallen on deaf ears. He knew that by their quick and immediate response.

"Therefore they were seeking again to seize Him, and He eluded their grasp" (John 10:39).

The Jews thought they had Him trapped at last! They had all heard those blasphemous statements. Surely He knew what they could do under God's Law. They couldn't have been blamed for obeying those Laws! He had read their minds and also knew the Scripture they considered. It had placed Him in whatever category they chose. He was considered, by them, as either a Jew or an alien.

"Moreover, the one who blasphemes the name of the Lord shall surely be put to death; all the congregation shall certainly stone him. The alien as well as the native, when he blasphemes the Name, shall be put to death" (Leviticus 24:16).

There was one big problem they faced. They were unable to persuade all the Jews for that. In their moment of hesitation and uncertainty, Jesus escaped stoning.

They had decided to return to their primary effort. They proceeded to plan how to arrest Him. They would let the Sanhedrin resolve the blasphemy. The Sanhedrin knew how to declare a man guilty. The Jews just had to present a strong case against Him. Jesus knew the people were divided about His guilt. He escaped the Jewish leaders to resume

His Mission. He had seen His coming suffering on the horizon. He could not have waited for their solution.

The Pharisees used an age-old strategy. (If you want to break a strong chain, look for the weakest link.) They had searched and discovered the weakest follower Jesus had. It was no accident. All had happened by a design. The Father had known what would happen to His Son.

Two days before the Passover Jesus knew the plot was laid. He had told His disciples of the coming crucifixion. The Jews had intended to use legal trickery.

"Then the chief priests and the elders of the people were gathered together in the court of the high priest, named Caiaphas; and they plotted together to seize Jesus by stealth, and kill Him. But they were saying, "Not during the festival, lest a riot occur among the people" (Matthew 26:3-5).

They were pleased when Caiaphas agreed to kill Jesus. They had not known that it presented a prophecy. Words of the prophecy had come from an unbelieving heart. God had used Caiaphas because of his position and not for his attitude. Almost like Baalim and Balik, his words had brought truth. They had said and planned everything God had expected of them. Had not God planned to fulfill His total plan and purpose?

"But a certain one of them, Caiaphas, who was high priest that year, said to them, "You know nothing at all, nor do you take into account that it is expedient for you that one man should die for the people, and that the whole nation should not perish." Now this he did not say on his own initiative; but being high priest that year, he prophesied that Jesus was going to die for the nation, and not for the nation only, but that He might also gather

together into one the children of God who are scat-
tered abroad. So from that day on they planned
together to kill Him" (John 11:49-53).

They had all agreed on the plan to kill Jesus. After all, He was just a meddlesome outsider. He hadn't attended any of the Rabbi Schools. He had to be ignorant of the Law and religious matters. Before He came, they had fully controlled the people. They were all so happy and fully sure of their success. They were glad they didn't try to just arrest Him. They had wanted His blood since the healing on the Sabbath.

Caiaphas and the chief priests had not anticipated that unexpected help. They were unprepared to be confronted by the weakest link in the equation.

"Then one of the twelve, named Judas Iscariot,
went to the chief priests, and said, "What are you
willing to give me to deliver Him up to you?" And
they weighed out to him thirty pieces of silver. And
from then on he began looking for a good oppor-
tunity to betray Him" (Matthew 26:14-16).

We didn't know how or when Judas planned to betray Him. There had to be some hidden reason to betray His teacher. His teacher was always very alert and awake to danger. He had to find some unique and clever plan. He was not weak and deceptive when joining the twelve. Jesus fully knew those He had chosen. There had to be something that caused him to change. Sometime during discipleship service he was overwhelmed with the temptation and succumbed.

"But Judas Iscariot, one of His disciples, who was
intending to betray Him, said, "Why was this per-
fume not sold for three hundred denarii and given
to the poor?" Now he said this, not because he was
concerned about the poor, but because he was a

thief, and as he had the money box, he used to pil-
fer what was put into it" (John 12:4-6).

The chief priests had discovered the link they needed. They now had the plan complete for trapping Jesus. They had a spy in the disciples' camp. They were laughing up their sleeves. Their efforts had finally borne fruit. They had acquired the help of their informer.

"Now the chief priests and the Pharisees had
given orders that if anyone knew where He was, he
should report it, that they might seize Him"
(John 11:57).

They needed someone who had definite knowledge of that blasphemer. That was the only way their plan had a chance. Regular Jews had never ignored or opposed their other decrees. All Jews feared the religious leaders. The three parties, Pharisees, Sadducees and Herodians, were to be respected. Any religious party felt threatened by Jesus' mission and miracles.

Jesus decided to avoid great crowds after the Passover. He had always spoken openly, whether in a synagogue or a temple or a village. Everywhere He went you found the crowds! His faithfully trained disciples were always by His side. They had known everything about His actions. They had slept where He did. They had eaten where He ate. They had prayed where He prayed. Disciples were always present with their Teacher! His mission was not destined to end by a premature mistake. Why? Because He knew the hearts of all people.

It was divine wisdom that caused Him to face the last threat. The "Hour of Suffering" was very near. He had permission to properly close His earthly mission. He showed how nothing was accidental to Him.

"For this reason the Father loves Me, because I
lay down My life that I may take it again. No one

has taken it from Me, but I lay it down on My own initiative. I have authority to lay it down, and I have authority to take it up again. This commandment I received from My Father" (John 10:17, 18).

He was ready to surrender to His enemies through God's plan. As He faced planned suffering, He experienced some consolation. Many of the Jews believed in His words and His miracles.

"Nevertheless many even of the rulers believed in Him, but because of the Pharisees they were not confessing Him, lest they should be put out of the synagogue; for they loved the approval of men rather than the approval of God" (John 12:42, 43).

The focus was upon Judas Iscariot, one of Jesus' disciples. The religious leaders' joy knew no limits. They were hardly able to constrain themselves! Judas probably knew all about Jesus. He was able to get closer to Jesus than they could. Satan had known of the Sanhedrin's plot. He was ready for any kind of evil. Judas was totally ignorant of the total evil plan. (We discovered that later.)

We had quite a workable combination in the arresting plan. We had a greedy disciple and bloodthirsty leaders. But they only wanted Jesus' blood. They had counted on Judas' law-abiding actions. They figured, like every man, he had his price. Judas was definitely their "key" man for betrayal. What reward had they planned to offer? How about thirty pieces of silver? They had no intention of telling everything. He had to feel that the arrest was all they had wanted. That way he had value as their best source of "help."

Was there an underlying reason for Judas helping the Jews? Had he, deep down, entertained a hatred for Jesus? According to one scripture, his motive involved some dishonest actions. Look again at the Gospel of John.

"...but because he was a thief, and as he had the money box, he used to pilfer what was put into it" (John 12:6).

How much had he stolen over those three years? How much had he misused? Was this not a good opportunity to redeem himself? He didn't want Jesus to discover his weakness and sin. Had his actions appeared law-abiding and their reward justified? Was the "reward" they offered him enough to cover the shortage? No doubt his Teacher had forgiveness ready for his sin. Why didn't he go to Him and confess? He had seen how Jesus had forgiven others. Jesus had forgiven unbelief but not rejection or betrayal.

The "Hour" for His suffering has begun. His enemies were readied for their successful plan. In His last teaching with the disciples He mentioned Father support. Without that support He had lost all needed strength for His suffering. This was the second time He mentioned Father support and presence. We believed it the first time He spoke.

"Jesus therefore said, "When you lift up the Son of Man, then you will know that I am He, and I do nothing on My own initiative, but I speak these things as the Father taught Me. And He who sent Me is with Me; He has not left Me alone, for I always do the things that are pleasing to Him." As He spoke these things, many came to believe in Him" (John 8:28-30).

The end result showed that true faith in His words. We are not talking about denominational doctrine or creed! We are not talking about some great theologian's concept or interpretation! We are talking about a simple faith acceptance of "His Words!"

Jesus accepted His inevitable coming suffering and nothing has changed. He has the same Father! He is the same Son!

He has not disappointed or disobeyed His Father! So, He made that second statement of His Father's support and presence. Are we to believe what "He" said or what "theologians" thought He meant? You have to decide as you allow His Spirit to bring truth. Now hear those actual words of Jesus.

"Behold, an hour is coming, and has already come, for you to be scattered, each to his own home, and to leave Me alone; and yet I am not alone because the Father is with Me" (John 16:32).

You must ask yourself that searching question. Could He have withstood all His suffering without the Father? If you are not sure, wait until the "Hour" is finished. You will then have the only correct answer!

Jesus was prepared as He waited for the unfolding plan. He knew Judas was the culprit being used. Notice what happened at the Passover supper.

"When Jesus had said this, He became troubled in spirit, and testified, and said, "Truly, truly, I say to you, that one of you will betray Me" (John 13:21).

When questioned by His disciples for the person's identity, Jesus made the reply.

"Jesus therefore answered, "That is the one for whom I shall dip the morsel and give it to him." So when He had dipped the morsel, He took and gave it to Judas, the son of Simon Iscariot. And after the morsel, Satan then entered into him. Jesus therefore said to him, "What you do, do quickly." Now no one of those reclining at the table knew for what purpose He had said this to him. For some were supposing, because Judas had the money box, that Jesus was saying to him, "Buy the things we have need of for the feast;" or else, that he should give something to the poor" (John 13:26-29).

The deal had been made in advance of the Supper. Judas knew what he was going to do. The disciples were not aware of the betrayal and impending suffering. Jesus' arrest had finally been realized by His enemies. Judas had known the Teacher's garden spot for prayer. He was the leader for the Roman officers and priest's henchmen. He understood that they just wanted to arrest Him. Oh, how he had been deceived! He imagined his importance would be acquired by leading the arresting group. The people had to notice his cooperation with the Sanhedrin. Judas knew his Teacher didn't believe in violence. After all, didn't He come to bring peace to mankind?

Evil always works better at night. The setting had been arranged. A most appropriate time for a betrayal when faces can't be recognized. Of course, in that Garden of Eden it had been light. But evil never stated that conditions had to be exact. It made its own conditions as they unfolded.

"Now Judas also, who was betraying Him, knew the place; for Jesus had often met there with His disciples" (John 18:2).

Judas experienced a mental awakening! Why had they brought their weapons? They knew Jesus wasn't armed or possessed weapons. During the darkest part of night, before dawn, Judas led them.

"Judas then, having received the Roman cohort, and officers from the chief priests and Pharisees, came there with lanterns and torches and weapons" (John 18:3).

What a spectacle was presented! His enemies had their best weapons, plenty of light, and political help. Had Judas lied and told them Jesus was hiding? He knew their plans long before they appeared. He could have moved to a different location. Had He wanted them to find and arrest

Him? The Jews had persuaded the Romans that Jesus caused trouble. It was easy to get Roman cooperation for that plan. It was made impossible for Him to resist arrest. That was the conclusion in the mind of the Pharisees.

"Jesus therefore, knowing all the things that were coming upon Him, went forth, and said to them, "Whom do you seek?" (John 18:4).

He was not bodily and forcefully dragged from a hiding place! He was not flushed out like some criminal or wild animal. Look again what we observed. He knew they were coming. He also knew His "Hour of Suffering" began.

We are faced with an action mentioned by the other gospels. The Gospel of John omitted that action. What was it? The kiss of the betrayer. Its acceptance or omission did not change Jesus' Mission. Since it was very dark, was a pre-arranged signal necessary? Was not the writer of John's Gospel an eyewitness? Would he not have known all that happened? Look what that Gospel account stated. Jesus stepped forth to confront them. He hadn't needed Judas' supposed important kiss. The Pharisees didn't need Judas to identify Jesus. There was plenty of light for them to recognize Him. Was not Judas a useless pawn in their game?

"They answered Him, "Jesus the Nazarene." He said to them, "I am He." And Judas also who was betraying Him, was standing with them. When therefore He said to them, "I am He," they drew back and fell to the ground" (John 18:5, 6).

It was very obvious that Judas had chosen the wrong crowd. Isn't that always what happens when the deceived discover the truth?

The soldiers had concluded that Jesus was a criminal. They were prepared to act accordingly. Their orders were to prepare for defensive action. Had the religious leaders hoped Jesus would resist? If the soldiers killed Him, their problem was solved. They had no concern if He were "accidentally" killed.

Take another look at the Gethsemane arrest. The Scripture didn't tell us which group led the action. It had seemed logical to identify those who fell back. His words had no meaning to the Roman soldiers. That was proven hours later. We had to conclude that temple officers and chief priests fell back. They were those who really were afraid of Jesus' power and popularity. They were amazed and confused that He boldly confronted them. Soldiers usually only feared those enemies who had weapons. Besides, what had the soldiers feared from a religious fanatic?

Take that last look at the garden activity. When Jesus "went forth," Judas lost his importance and effectiveness. Why? Because Jesus had surprised the chief priests and Judas by His actions. They hadn't expected His attitude of fearlessness! Jesus didn't allow a secret signal to finish His arrest. Had not Judas really been betrayed by the Pharisees? After they had recovered from His bold statement, He spoke.

"Again therefore He asked them, "Whom do you seek?" And they said, "Jesus the Nazarene." Jesus answered, "I told you that I am He; if therefore you seek me, let these go their way," that the word might be fulfilled which He spoke, "Of those who Thou hast given Me I lost not one" (John 18:7-9).

The stage had been set, all the arrest plans are finished. His religious and political enemies proceeded to follow their orders.

"So the Roman cohort and the commander and the officers of the Jews, arrested Jesus and bound Him, and led Him to Annas first; for he was father-

in-law of Caiaphas, who was high priest that year" (John 18:12, 13).

The high priests proceeded to question Jesus concerning His disciples and teaching. After brief questions, Annas left Him bound and sent Him to Caiaphas. From the high priest, Caiaphas, they took Him to the Praetorium. That was where Pilate the governor lived. The Jews didn't enter the governor's residence. That would have defiled them. They would have been unable to eat the Passover. So Pilate went outside.

"Pilate therefore went out to them, and said, "What accusation do you bring against this Man?" They answered and said to him, "If this Man were not an evildoer, we would not have delivered Him up to you" (John 18:29, 30).

Pilate knew that the problem was Jewish and not Roman. He had not heard any disturbance caused by that Teacher. He had to act quickly. He didn't consider getting involved in religious problems. That wasn't his field of operations. Of course he knew that the Jewish Sanhedrin handled religious issues.

"Pilate therefore said to them, "Take Him your-selves, and judge Him according to your law." The Jews said to him, "We are not permitted to put any-one to death." That the words of Jesus might be fulfilled, which He spoke, signifying by what kind of death He was about to die" John 18:31, 32).

The Jewish priests had lied to Pilate. They were allowed to put someone to death. Their Law allowed them to use stoning but not crucifixion. Crucifixion was primarily the method of punishment used by Romans.

"Pilate therefore entered again into the Praetorium, and summoned Jesus, and said to Him, "Are You the

King of the Jews?" Jesus answered, "Are you say-
ing this on your own initiative, or did others tell you
about Me?" (John 18:33, 34).

The chief priests had said that to Pilate about Jesus. Of course Jesus knew those were the exact words they used. Why? They had to make the crime political against Jesus.

We must take note here of very important information. It is related to the term: "King of the Jews." After King Herod's death in 4 B.C.E., there were problems about ruling. Herod Antipas wanted to be called King of the Jews. Caesar Augustus did not allow it. After Caesar Augustus died, Antipas tried to become King of the Jews. He tried that in the late 20's C.E. but failed. That title then fell to Herod Agrippi I. Finally, Herod the Great was King of the Jews from 37-4 B.C.E. Now you understand the problem that seemed to confuse the Magi.

The chief priests mentioned the old issue that offended the Jews. They had never wanted a Roman king or ruler. Jesus, as King, would be no threat to Jewish people. He was a severe threat only to the ruling Pharisees. Pilate answered Jesus' question with two more vivid questions.

"Pilate therefore said to Him, "What is truth?"
And when he had said this, he went out again to
the Jews and said to them, "I find no guilt in Him.
But you have a custom that I should release some-
one for you at the Passover; do you wish then that
I release for you the King of the Jews?"
(John 18:38, 39).

They all, with one voice wanted Pilate to release Barabbas. Hearing their reply, Pilate took Jesus and had Him scourged.

Pilate definitely had the opportunity to free Jesus. He made a clear statement about His innocence. He was a very careful local ruler. Maybe he could have partially appeased the bloodthirsty mob. Aren't religious leaders supposed to show some mercy? Wasn't there someone who had pity for Him? He's taken away! It's too late for Him! The people didn't seem to be concerned about His punishment. The Roman soldiers were ready with their cruelty and hatred for criminals. They were experienced in causing pain!

The "Hour of Suffering" had been initiated by His arrest. The scourging marked the second phase of His suffering. What was the first phase? Being cruelly snatched from His beloved disciples and other believers. The soldiers' mockery and insults for Jesus seemed irregular. Why? Was that because He had been a "religious" leader? It was obvious the Roman soldiers had not acted alone. They were only under orders. Pilate could have changed the scourging order with one command.

We knew a criminal received scourging after being sentenced to crucifixion. But wait! Something was wrong! Jesus didn't have a Roman trial for His "crimes." Yet Pilate had Him scourged. All of that happened after Jesus had a mock trial before Caiaphas.

"And those who had seized Jesus led Him away to Caiaphas, the high priest, where the scribes and the elders were gathered together" (Matthew 26:57).

All the disciples had left Him and fled. He had to face His accusers alone. As the Teacher of Truth, He was expected to have many friends. He had healed many people! Where were they? What about those who saw Him perform miracles? All those who should have spoken for Him were silent. There He stood before Caiaphas.

"And the high priest stood up and said to Him, "Do You make no answer? What is it that these men are testifying against You?" But Jesus kept silent. And the high priest said to Him, "I adjure You by the

115

living God, that You tell us whether You are the Christ, the Son of God" (Matthew 26:62, 63).

What was He supposed to say? What did He have to say? He was the Father's messenger for truth. He could not do otherwise. When all others had lied about Him, they had known the truth. The high priest was not prepared for the answer He gave. God has always hated lies and His Son was no exception. Jesus openly admitted the truth of the high priest's statement. By doing that He had actually signed the Jews' death warrant.

"Jesus said to him, "You have said it yourself; nevertheless I tell you, hereafter you shall see 'THE SON OF MAN SITTING AT THE RIGHT HAND OF POWER, and COMING ON THE CLOUDS OF HEAVEN.'" Then the high priest tore his robes, saying, "He has blasphemed! What further need do we have of witnesses? Behold, you have now heard the blasphemy; what do you think?" They answered and said, "He is deserving of death!" (Matthew 26:64-66).

The following morning they bound Him and led Him away. They had all agreed to take Him to Pilate for sentencing. That was the last chance for Pilate even though he had help.

"When therefore they were gathered together, Pilate said to them, "Whom do you want me to release for you? Barabbas, or Jesus who is called Christ?" For he knew that because of envy they had delivered Him up. And while he was setting on the judgment seat, his wife sent to him, saying, "Have nothing to do with that righteous Man; for last night I suffered greatly in a dream because of Him" (Matthew 27:17-19).

Pilate totally ignored his wife's suggestion. He also ignored the answers he had received from Jesus. Pilate admitted he could find no fault in Jesus. He had spoken from the standpoint of breaking Roman law. But it was easier for him to try and avoid trouble. So he willingly submitted to the chief priests' evil desires. He had been put on the spot and had no moral convictions. Therefore, unfortunately, Jesus was sentenced by the Jews but punished by the Romans.

> *"Pilate said to them, "Then what shall I do with Jesus who is called the Christ?" They all said, "Let Him be crucified!" And he said, "Why, what evil has He done?" But they kept shouting all the more, saying, "Let Him be crucified!" And when Pilate saw that he was accomplishing nothing, but rather that a riot was starting, he took water and washed his hands in front of the multitude, saying, "I am innocent of this Man's blood; see to that yourselves." And all the people answered and said, "His blood be on us and our children!" (Matthew 27:22-25).*

That attempt by Pilate to release Jesus was in vain. The chief priests and people were a bloodthirsty bunch. He hoped that a little shed blood was all they needed. We all knew that wasn't enough for them at Jesus' crucifixion!

Did you ever witness a scourging? Pilate had seen his share. He never personally cared to watch. It was not a pleasant picture to see. Are YOU prepared for it?

> *"Then Pilate therefore took Jesus and scourged Him" (John 19:1).*

Scourging usually came before a crucifixion. The criminal was stripped of all his clothes. His hands were tied to the top of a four-foot post. His bowed back was exposed as the ordeal began. A two-foot long whip was used. It had a handle with strips of strong leather attached. At the end of the strips were tied pieces of bone or lead. The heavy lashes fell on the total back area of the criminals. The skin of the back was pulled tight while arched over the short post. The whip quickly sliced through flesh and muscle tissue! Sometimes chunks of flesh were snatched off with the whip!

The executioners had not known Jesus in a personal way. They were just doing as they were ordered. Since the whips were short, the men tired sooner. When one tired, another whip user took his place. Of course, the criminals had no "resting periods." The people kept watching as the lashes fell. Some even liked to count each lash. They felt a certain satisfaction as the blood started to flow! The executioners were very hard-hearted. They were trained to show no pity or mercy. Had they any reason to do so? Wasn't He just like any other criminal they had given lashes? Had this Jesus become the object of their hatred for all Jews? The Romans had no love for the Jewish nation and their leaders.

The number of lashes Jesus received was unknown to us. The Jews were only allowed to give forty lashes. They were also allowed to give thirty-nine several times. The Jews had carefully observed that admonition of Deuteronomy 25:3. That was proven later by the Apostle Paul. He stated the factual truth for us.

"Five times I received from the Jews thirty-nine lashes" (II Corinthians 11:24).

But, of course, the Romans could give as many as they desired. They had no moral code or religious law to obey.

That Teacher of Truth was not destined to die from scourging! He had to complete His Father's Mission! Many criminals died at the scourging post. Pilate wondered how long the Teacher would last! The crowd had hoped He would die quickly but painfully! The scene appeared to represent an event of the amphitheater! The only difference was that those people were cheering the "lions of Rome."

It would have been unthinkable to minimize His suffering. It would have been different if the Jewish method had been used. It would have been different if the scourging was the end. But wait! That was only the beginning of His agony. Greater agony was heaped upon that foundation of pain. Yet we know no Gospel writer described the scourging. All information was gleaned from historical sources. We know that the later martyrs were scourged with greater intensity. Many had their veins and body organs clearly exposed during scourging.

You have just viewed the greatest example of man's inhumanity to man! You had imagined the crowd applauding one man's excruciating pain! And yet that was only one third enough to please. Much more had to happen to satisfy their bloodthirst and hatred! Remember! Pilate was the real instigator of the whole happening.

We are not able to imagine the physical pain He suffered. How was anyone able to stand afterward? We know that many criminals died immediately before their crucifixion. Why was He able to stand after the scourging? He had also come to earth to fulfill other prophecy. Remember! He came to give His life as a ransom for many.

"He was despised and forsaken of men,
A man of sorrows, and acquainted with grief;
And like one from whom men hide their face, He
was despised, and we did not esteem Him.
Surely our griefs He Himself bore,
And our sorrows He carried;
Yet we ourselves esteemed Him stricken,
Smitten of God, and afflicted.
But He was pierced through for our transgressions,

119

He was crushed for our iniquities;
The chastening for our well-being fell upon Him,
And by His scourging we are healed"
(Isaiah 53:3-5).

After the scourging, the cruel hearted Roman soldiers mocked Him. They proceeded to treat Him like a king. They made a crown of two-inch thorns and placed it on His head. They found a purple robe and placed it around Him. They then proceeded to ridicule Him with blows to His face. While doing so they repeated the words, "Hail, King of the Jews."

"Jesus therefore came out, wearing the crown of thorns and the purple robe. And Pilate said to them, "Behold the Man!" When therefore the chief priests and the officers saw Him, they cried out saying, "Crucify, Crucify!" Pilate said to them, "Take Him yourselves, and crucify Him, for I find no guilt in Him." The Jews answered him, "We have a law, and by that law He ought to die because He made Himself out to be the Son of God" (John 19:5-7).

The executioners had not believed that Christ was really human. While they lashed Him, He did not curse them. While they lashed Him, He did not cry out. They were correct. He was not human only. He was human and divine. There had never lived a person on earth like Him! They had never understood Him because they lacked spiritual knowledge.

Pilate irritated the Jews by trying to assist Jesus' case. Their patience finally became exhausted. They then introduced a personal political threat he couldn't ignore.

"As a result of this Pilate made efforts to release Him, but the Jews cried out, saying, "If you release

this Man, you are no friend to Caesar; everyone who makes himself out to be a king opposes Caesar." Now it was the day of preparation for the Passover; it was about the sixth hour. And he said to the Jews, "Behold, your King!" They therefore cried out, "Away with Him, away with Him, crucify Him!" Pilate said to them, "Shall I crucify your King?" The chief priests answered, "We have no king but Caesar." So he then delivered Him to them to be crucified" (John 19:12-16).

We saw the soldiers lead Him to the place of crucifixion. Did He attempt to remove the crown of thorns? No! Did He throw off the purple robe? No! The purple robe covered His inner blood-soaked tunic. We don't know how much blood He had shed! See Him as He very painfully and slowly walked the distance. To be publicly taunted and abused was part of the shame. The criminal always traveled the same route and everyone knew it. He received no mercy from the crowds lining the way. There went the King of the Jews to His punishment!

Normally the person was forced to carry the horizontal section to the crucifixion site. The "cross" piece was tied on the person's shoulder to carry. How was the criminal able to have strength after the required scourging? The cross had two parts. The upright post stayed sunken in the ground. The crossbeam had weighed from 70 to 100 pounds. It was the criminal's job to carry the "crossbeam" only. It was shaped like the capital letter "I" turned horizontally.

The victim, severely weakened from the scourging, was expected to fall several times. When he fell forward, with hands tied to the "crossbeam," his face hit the cobblestones. When he fell backward, the back of his head hit the "crossbeam."

*"They took Jesus therefore, and He went out bear-
ing His own cross, to the place called the Peace of
a Skull, which in the Hebrew, (Jewish Aramaic) is
called Golgotha" (John 19:17).*

Many criminals, or Rome's enemies, were just kept tied
only and crucified. There, in their nakedness, they died
from exposure, shame, and agony of scourging. But they
planned the maximum for God's Son. They stripped the
blood-soaked tunic and robe from His body. That was normal procedure for any crucifixion. Wait! Had someone
given Him any food or water? NO! To have been withheld
food or water was a form of punishment. He had been
deprived of basic human kindness. What kind of creatures
were those chief priests to allow that?

He had finally and painfully reached the crucifixion
site. The soldiers laid Him on the ground. They stretched
His arms against the "crossbeam." They proceeded to
pound a spike into each wrist above the thumb. The spikes
were five to seven inches in length. They then raised Him,
nailed on the crossbeam, by ropes and secured Him to the
upright beam. A crude block of wood was nailed between
His legs. That probably kept His wrists secured longer to
the crossbeam. They finally fastened the feet to the upright
beam with spikes.

His body weight hanging by His arms caused a major
breathing problem. He could only properly exhale by push-
ing up on His spiked feet. After exhaling, His weight had
shifted to His arms again. He kept moving up and down to
avoid suffocation while trying to breathe. The constant
motion rubbed His lashed back against the upright beam.

There He was hanged and exposed to the greatest
shame and ridicule! In extreme pain and agony, the bodily
functions were uncontrollable. That was what caused

delight to the crowd present. They taunted Him as He was plagued by insects attracted to His bleeding. There was also no respite from the hot sun or rain. His arms had terrific and constant strain! His wrists and feet were swollen around the spikes! His head burned with the wound-caused fever! It seemed as though time had stopped! Every agonizing minute seemed an hour! His strength was quickly being drained from His body!

How long had He been crucified? He had lost all sense of time. Through all of that, He had not spoken against His enemies. Had He known there wasn't much longer to wait? His "Hour of Suffering" had moved to the planned finish. The Father knew His Son's earthly mission was finished. It had to be accomplished unto divine satisfaction.

There are those who erroneously believe that the Father forsook His Son. Those who do need some comparative Scripture study. Are we to accept theologians' interpretations or His Son's words? We first go to that Messianic Prophet who introduced the truth.

"But the Lord was pleased to crush Him, putting Him to grief; If He would render Himself as a guilt offering, He will see His offspring, He will prolong His days, and the good pleasure of the Lord will prosper in His hand. As a result of the anguish of His soul, He will see it and be satisfied; By His knowledge the Righteous One, My Servant, will justify the many as He will bear their iniquities" (Isaiah 53:10, 11).

We are sure that Isaiah was not speaking of David. Nor was he speaking of Israel. Was he not speaking of the Messiah? Was not Jesus, God's Son, the Messiah?

If you refused to believe Isaiah's identification, what about God's words? Did you remember the Father's comments about His Son? Would He have changed His opinion about His Son's actions? Remember His stamp of approval after Jesus submitted to baptism?

"And after being baptized, Jesus went up immedi-
ately from the water; and behold, the heavens were
opened, and He saw the Spirit of God descending
as a dove, and coming upon Him, and behold, a
voice out of the heavens, saying, "This is My
beloved Son, in whom I am well-pleased"
(Matthew 3:16-17).

We must quickly confirm the Father's words at His Son's Transfiguration. His stamp of approval seemed emphasized because of the occasion. Not only Jesus' disciples but all Jews needed that emphasis.

"And a voice came out of the cloud, saying, "This
is My Son, My chosen One, listen to Him!"
(Luke 9:35).

The stage had been set by Isaiah long before Jesus' birth. God had never spoken truth through a prophet then changed that truth. Since His Son claimed to be the Truth, hear Him speak! Not just once but several times. First, hear some words every father needs to hear.

"And He who sent Me is with Me; He has not left
Me alone, for I always do the things that are pleas-
ing to Him." As He spoke these things, many came
to believe in Him" (John 8:29, 30).

As He faced His finished mission, His "divine" relationship remains. He knew the disciples' fear of worldly persecution was strong.

"Behold, an hour is coming, and has already come,
for you to be scattered, each to his own home, and
to leave Me alone; and yet I am not alone, because
the Father is with Me" (John 16:32).

Was that a lie from the One claiming to be the truth? Or, what He had spoken was really the truth? Consider that very carefully! He was the Truth. The Messianic Prophet spoke the truth! The Heavenly Father spoke the truth! The Son of God spoke the truth. Therefore, any explanation that contradicts these "truths" is non-comparative interpretation.

We cannot parallel any other biblical characters with Jesus. He stands in a class all by Himself. Why not consider His spoken words accordingly? The most important ones concern those at the crucifixion. The four gospel writers separate all the sayings of Jesus. They are listed here for your comparison and analysis.

Luke alone showed God's forgiveness to the soldiers. We don't know why the others failed to record it.

"But Jesus was saying, "Father forgive them; for they do not know what they are doing." AND THEY CAST LOTS, DIVIDING UP HIS GARMENTS AMONG THEMSELVES" (Luke 23:34).

Only the Gospel of John gives an extensive account of Jesus' garments.

"The soldiers therefore, when they had crucified Jesus, took His outer garments and made four parts, a part to every soldier and also the tunic; now the tunic was seamless, woven in one piece. They said therefore to one another, "Let us not tear it, but cast lots for it, to decide whose it shall be;" that the Scripture might be fulfilled, "THEY DIVIDED MY OUTER GARMENTS AMONG THEM, AND FOR MY CLOTHING THEY CAST LOTS" (John 19:23, 24).

Luke again stands alone concerning the obvious destiny of one criminal. Let's interrupt his words, to the other criminal, about Jesus' innocence.

"And we indeed justly, for we are receiving what we deserve for our deeds; but this man has done nothing wrong." And he was saying, "Jesus, remember me when You come in Your kingdom!" And He said to him, "Truly I say to you, today you shall be with Me in Paradise" (Luke 23:41-43).

The above words were spoken shortly before the sixth hour. That is found recorded in the scriptures. Luke and John seemed designated as personally witnessing these events. Since that was so, we focus on their crucifixion record.

Why do most believers and preachers omit the crucifixion positives? Why do not Matthew and Mark record the positives of Luke and John? Was it because they didn't see the larger picture? Hear John's Gospel as he alone records those words. These are all positives!

"After this, Jesus, knowing that all things had already been accomplished, in order that the Scripture might be fulfilled, said, "I am thirsty" (John 19:28).

Luke then reveals the words spoken shortly afterward. All of these are positive and hopeful for all mankind.

"And Jesus, crying out with a loud voice, said, "Father, INTO THY HANDS I COMMIT MY SPIRIT." And having said this, He breathed His last" (Luke 23:46).

John echoes the above words with that positive divine finality! We will find his words later in his account. Both accounts form a most powerful testimony.

Jesus' life was never lived with a defeatist attitude. We know He always obeyed the Heavenly Father! We know He always pleased His Father! There is Scripture recorded of efforts to stone Him. Why couldn't they stone Him? Why couldn't they have crucified Him earlier? Was it not obvious that God protected and spared His life? Was His life not under God's providential protection?

There was a translation of the Gospels and the Psalms discovered early in the 1950's. It is the Holy Bible from the Peshitta. It was translated by George M. Lamsa. It is the authorized Bible of the Church of the East. Aramaic was the language of the Church that spread east. The Gospel message was first preached in the Aramaic of the Jews and Christians. In the first century, Jesus and His earlier followers spoke Aramaic. Of course, they also knew Hebrew.

The Israelites never wrote their sacred literature in any language but Aramaic and Hebrew, which are sister languages. There is no proof that Jesus and His disciples could converse in Greek. We don't know if they ever heard Greek spoken.

Only by using the Peshitta translation from the Aramaic do we find the positive Messiah. The Gospel of Luke and of John would agree with the Aramaic of Matthew and Mark. Both of those writers, Matthew 27:46 and Mark 15:34 agree on the translation. There is no variance in word usage. They both record Jesus' words:

> "Eli, Eli, lemana shabakthani! Which means My God, My God, for this I was spared" (Matthew 27:46). This was my destiny. (By A.J. HOLMAN COMPANY 1957. Copyright 1933, 1939, and 1940.) p. 986.

His mouth was hot and dry. He received the signal from the Father. He accepted the sponge soaked with vinegar. Now He had some moisture in His mouth. He mustered all His remaining strength for those words. The soldiers had heard Him. Was that part of the Father's plan? Were not the soldiers waiting for Him to die? That cheap wine in the sponge did the job. It did not have a sedative effect! It did not dull His senses! He still knew fully what He was doing. His Heavenly Father had provided the temporary "refreshing" He needed. He spoke those words to spiritually refresh all mankind!

"I am thirsty" (John 19:28).

The numberless host of heaven then waited for that finale! The first three words, a divine number, were spoken. All of heaven heard them! It's as though a great silence is felt in heaven. Then suddenly the soldiers see His lips move again.

"When Jesus therefore had received the sour wine, He said, "It is finished!" And He bowed His head, and gave up His spirit" (John 19:30).

That same divine number of words was spoken for us. He had fully completed His mission for all mankind! Was that not what the high priest had predicted?

"Now this he did not say on his own initiative; but being high priest that year, he prophesied that Jesus was going to die for the nation; and not for the nation only, but that He might also gather together into one the children of God who are scattered abroad" (John 11:51, 52).

Caiaphas was right about Jesus' suffering and death. But, of course, not just for the Jewish nation. His suffering and death were God's way for uniting all His believers!

Who had suffered and died on that day? Who was that Jewish Messiah God had provided for mankind? John gave us the answer in his Gospel beginning.

"The next day he saw Jesus coming to him, and said, "Behold, the Lamb of God who takes away the sin of the world!" (John 1:29).

There's the answer we were all waiting to hear. Pilate could not have stopped His Mission! The Jews could not have

128

stopped His mission! The soldiers had been allowed a part in His finale! Why? Because He did not come to fail! Why, primarily? Because God had "spared" His Son for this "Hour!"

Every aspect of His Life Mission was kept distinctly intact. We saw that His robe was kept whole. Why? Because it was woven in one piece. His body, both prophetically and actually, had no broken bones. Not even small breaks! The soldiers' lack of procedure gave us actual, after death proof!

> *"The soldiers therefore came, and broke the legs of the first man, and of the other man who was crucified with Him; but coming to Jesus, when they saw that He was already dead, they did not break His legs; but one of the soldiers pierced His side with a spear, and immediately there came out blood and water" (John 19:32-34).*

Now we deal with the prophetic truth that awaited us. Why? Because God left out nothing for doubters or unbelievers.

> *"For these things came to pass, that the Scripture might be fulfilled, "NOT A BONE OF HIM SHALL BE BROKEN." And again another Scripture says, "THEY SHALL LOOK ON HIM WHOM THEY PIERCED" (John 19:36, 37).*

And so was completed every planned segment of God's plan.

Two of His recent Jewish disciples, Joseph of Arimathea and Nicodemus, took His body down. They bound it in linen wrappings, with spices, as was the custom of the Jews.

> *"Now in the place where He was crucified there was a garden; and in the garden a new tomb, in which no one had been laid. Therefore on account of the Jewish day of preparation, because the tomb was nearby, they laid Jesus there" (John 19:41, 42).*

It was over! He was gone! His cross is empty and His grave is occupied! Did He fail in that last Hour? Had He possessed a weakness that finally defeated Him? Had the Father forced something upon His Son for our sakes? We had to say no to all of that! Why? Because He never surrendered out of human weakness or uncertainty! Hear the truth echo to us from His past humanity. He spoke of that same love He showed us at Golgotha!

"For this reason the Father loves Me, because I lay down My life that I may take it again. No one has taken it away from Me, but I lay it down of My own initiative. I have authority to lay it down, and I have authority to take it up again. This commandment I received from My Father"
(John 10:17, 18).

There is the answer that's adequate for any human being. It is God's truth whether or not one believes it!

This "Hour" had finished His earthly human life. Now we must find all the answers about His life's events. How could one believe that life does not end at the grave? If you are not sure, follow the resulting discoveries from His death. Remember, time is not under man's control! Is there Life after Death anywhere? The answer to that question has been made available. Only true believers in Him will understand!

We are dealing here with divine time not human time. Quickly! Stop the flowing and notice His "Hour" of Glory!

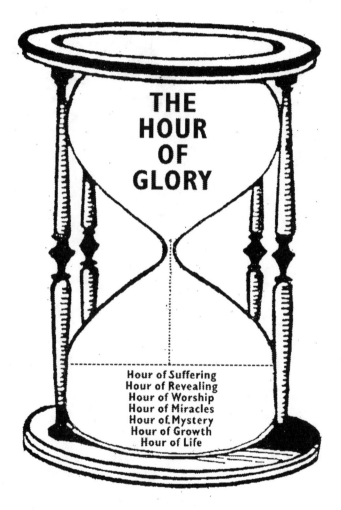

THE
HOUR
OF
GLORY

Hour of Suffering
Hour of Revealing
Hour of Worship
Hour of Miracles
Hour of Mystery
Hour of Growth
Hour of Life

HIS GLORIOUS DEATH

Chapter Eight

THE HOUR OF GLORY

We had been seeing God's Glory in His Son's life. This had been evident from the start of His Mission. There is much proof in Scripture to support that truth. The Gospel of John introduced that Glory to mankind. He was the only Gospel writer to emphasize the Pre-existent Son. We cannot continue without the origin of His Glory!

"And the Word became flesh and dwelt among us, and we beheld His Glory, glory as of the only begotten from the Father, full of grace and truth" (John 1:14).

Anything the Son did had manifested God's Glory. Whether it was teaching, healing, or performing miracles to help mankind. And so, His "Hour" of Glory began with His teaching. What did His teaching involve? The fulfillment of prophesy and the purpose of His Mission.

"And He began teaching in their synagogues and was praised by all. And He came to Nazareth, where

133

He had been brought up; and as was His custom, He entered the synagogue on the Sabbath, and stood up and read. And the book of the prophet Isaiah was handed to Him. And He opened the Book, and found the place where it was written, THE SPIRIT OF THE LORD IS UPON ME, BECAUSE HE ANOINTED ME TO PREACH THE GOSPEL TO THE POOR. HE HAS SENT ME TO PROCLAIM RELEASE TO THE CAPTIVES, AND RECOVERY OF SIGHT TO THE BLIND, TO SET FREE THOSE WHO ARE DOWNTRODDEN, TO PROCLAIM THE ACCEPTABLE YEAR OF THE LORD. And He closed the book, and gave it back to the attendant, and sat down; and the eyes of all the synagogue were fixed on Him. And He began to say to them, "Today this Scripture has been fulfilled in your hearing" (Luke 4:15-21).

We know that His teachings proclaimed God's power and authority. He never drew attention to Himself by any means He possessed. Remember the time His teaching was emphasized with a "necessary" miracle? That was solely to help mankind! He was not trying to "get" glory. He had just fed a multitude of people. Notice their intentions after He was finished.

"When therefore the people saw the sign which He had performed, they said, "This is of a truth the Prophet who is to come into the world." Jesus therefore perceiving that they were intending to come and take Him by force, to make Him king, withdrew again to the mountain by Himself alone" (John 6:14, 15).

They wanted to make Him a king. What was wrong with that? Would not the Son of God have been their best choice? Wouldn't He have received glory in being King of Israel? But what purpose had they in wanting to make Him king? Was it not just to have kept their stomachs full? He would not have been their king just for that. That was not His primary purpose or Mission. It was not the time to tell them.

His "hour" of Glory actually began with His first miracle. As then, and every time thereafter, a miracle was purposeful. It encouraged people to believe in His Heavenly Father. Did you remember the wine miracle at the only wedding feast recorded?

"This beginning of His signs Jesus did in Cana of Galilee, and manifested His glory, and His disciples believed in Him" (John 2:11).

That pattern of action had to continue throughout His ministry. It was confronted wherever He was present. That pattern became most obvious when dealing with Martha's dead brother.

"Jesus said to her, "Did I not say to you, if you believe, you will see the glory of God?"
(John 11:40).

Notice another study of His "hour" of Glory. Rather than the "hour is coming," we hear the "hour has come." There was still that divine time element involved. He had to refer to it as current or futuristic. We had found that as a reference to His death. That was proof He had to physically die to be glorified!

"And Jesus answered them, saying, "The hour has come for the Son of Man to be glorified. Now My soul has become troubled; and what shall I say, "Father, save Me from this hour? But for this purpose I came to this hour. Father, glorify Thy name." There came therefore a voice out of

heaven: "I have both glorified it, and will glorify
it again" (John 12:23, 27, 28).

It sounded like He asked permission to omit that "hour." Of course that was not true. His next statement confirmed it. The Father did not misunderstand His Son's request. He was sure the Father would guarantee His success. That was emphasized in the last part of verse twenty-seven. The very core of Jesus' Mission was "glory" to God.

He knew that to be glorified must be preceded by His suffering. We had no doubt about that from what He said. There was no other interpretation to understand His divine purpose. He said, a grain of wheat if it dies, it bears much fruit. He had full assurance from God that glory awaited Him! He had spoken in John 10:18 of being given full authority. His Father had never decreased or recalled any of it!

He was perfect, sinless man, as well as God. In John 12, He called Himself Son of Man. He had used that title ten times in John's Gospel. Why? Because He had been born for mankind. He alone was designated as the Sacrifice for mankind's sins. He came to be identified with you and me! He tried to alert and notify Nicodemus of His willingness. He had pointed to His suffering and crucifixion as necessary pre-conditions. He tried to make it clear to Pharisees. But sometimes our physical "sight" hinders that spiritual faith "seeing." That law abiding Jewish teacher lacked the deepest Scriptural truth. His faith "sight" had to be opened!

"If I told you earthly things and you do not believe,
how shall you believe if I tell you of heavenly
things?" And as Moses lifted up the serpent in the
wilderness, even so must the Son of Man be lifted
up; that whosoever believes may in Him have eter-
nal life" (John 3:12, 14, 15).

Again, we saw why the multitudes sought the Son of Man. He had known their minds and hearts concerning Him.

"Jesus answered them and said, "Truly, truly, I say to you, you seek Me, not because you saw signs, but because you ate of the loaves, and were filled. Do not work for the food which perishes, but for the food which endures to eternal life, which the Son of Man shall give to you, for on Him the Father, even God, has set His seal" (John 6:26, 27).

That One on whom God set His Seal was Glorified! Jesus kept emphasizing that to the Pharisees and multitudes alike. He always wanted them to remember what preceded His glory. Why didn't they understand the Father's purpose in His Son's Mission? How could they have been so dense?

"Jesus therefore said, "When you lift up the Son of Man, then you will know that I am He, and I do nothing on My own initiative, but I speak these things as the Father taught Me" (John 8:28).

We conclude John's reference to the Son of Man. Jesus made that last attempt for the benefit of the multitude. They had just heard the Father's voice sound from heaven. But they did not associate that sound with His Father. That Messiah clearly identified His crucifixion, but their minds had been darkened.

"And I, if I be lifted up from the earth, will draw all men to Myself." But He was saying this to indicate the kind of death by which He was to die. The multitude therefore answered Him, "We have heard out of the Law that the Christ is to remain forever; and how can You say, "The Son of Man must be lifted up? Who is this Son of Man?" (John 12:32-34).

The "king" idea erupted after the "loaves and fish" miracle. Not long after that He had raised a dead man. Nothing

137

was able to stop the multitude. He became their prime candidate for Israel's "king." It reminded one of another time in Israel's history. We all recall when Israel wanted Saul of Kish for their king. God allowed them to choose him against the divine desire. Their choice was from physical appearance mainly. Here they try to make history repeat itself. At His triumphal entry into Jerusalem they treated Him like a king. Remember how He said that was His destiny? Not too long after His triumphal entry, He had said that to Pilate.

> *"On the next day the great multitude who had come to the feast, when they heard that Jesus was coming to Jerusalem, took the branches of the palm trees, and went out to meet Him, and began to cry out, "HOSANNA! BELESSED IS HE WHO COMES IN THE NAME OF THE LORD, even the King of Israel." And Jesus finding a young donkey, sat on it; as it is written, "FEAR NOT, DAUGHTER OF ZION; BEHOLD, YOUR KING IS COMING, SEATED ON A DONKEY'S COLT." These things His disciples did not understand at the first; but when Jesus was glorified, then they remembered that these things were written of Him, and that they had done these things to Him"*
> *(John 12:12-16).*

We realized, as above, He was always fulfilling prophecy. But the multitude had incorrectly understood the triumphal entry. They did correctly use "Hosanna" but He could not be King of Israel. He could not have completed His Mission as Israel's King. Why not? He had come to be mankind's Redeemer, not just a special nation's King.

Mankind had waited centuries for a unique redeemer. God purposed that they should wait no longer. His Chosen

People had been visited by God's Messiah. Almost thirty-three years had passed. God was now ready to glorify His Son. The glorification had only one obstacle for completion. His Son had to endure the suffering of His Crucifixion. Then it had happened! His Son was crucified and had died. The "Glory" His Son was promised had already been granted! Mankind's "salvation plan" had been completed! Yet, at the same time, He received His proper King title. He was proclaimed, by His death, His own people's supreme title.

"And Pilate wrote an inscription also, and put it on the cross. And it was written, JESUS THE NAZARENE, THE KING OF THE JEWS. And so the chief priests of the Jews were saying to Pilate, "Do not write, 'The King of the Jews;' but that He said, 'I am King of the Jews.'" Pilate answered, "What I have written I have written"
(John 19:19, 21, 22).

In a way, the local government had made Him "King" of the Jews. Ironic, wasn't it? The Jews wanted Him killed to erase Him from their history. But His sacrifice for their sins made Him their King! Not only the Jewish people but Gentiles were also amazed. Both groups had heard about and seen His miracles. They weren't ever done in secret. We knew that the miracles enhanced the greatness of His Mission. Without miracles, His task would have been incomplete. With the "miracle factor," His life was remembered and glorified!

The time had come for the Gentiles to be included. Was not His salvation also for them? He expected them to have heard about His crucifixion. After all, that had become a national event, or spectacle! Every citizen, Jew or Gentile, witnessed those punishments. The Gentiles, or Greeks, also had to be involved before His glorification. We don't know how many had witnessed His crucifixion. Although, they had to have heard about His triumphal entry!

"Now there were certain Greeks among those who were going up to worship at the feast; these therefore came to Philip, who was from Bethsaida of Galilee, and began to ask him, saying, "Sir, we wish to see Jesus" (John 12:20, 21).

Immediately after that visit, Jesus had spoken about being glorified.

We don't know to whom He spoke the words about the "Son of Man" being glorified. No one knows how many Jews and Greeks were present. Could not the Gentiles have been quicker to have believed? Maybe they had already believed in His miracles. They also needed a Redeemer for their sins. They needed to personally hear Him speak. The Jews had but failed to believe Him. If Gentiles accepted Him as God's Messiah, He would become God's "Lamb" for their sins also. The disciples had heard His teachings for almost three years. In Matthew's Gospel account, He seemed to omit all Jews. Notice Jesus' orders to His disciples.

"These twelve Jesus sent out after instructing them, saying, "Do not go in the way of the Gentiles, and do not enter any city of the Samaritans; but rather go to the lost sheep of the house of Israel" (Matthew 10:5, 6).

How strange it was before the crucifixion. The Jews had deliberately chosen to refuse that Jesus. The outsiders, the Gentiles, had gone to seek Him. Wasn't that what God had intended from the very first? The Old Covenant was strictly Jewish. The Gentiles were not obligated to keep its strict provisions. So, according to divine agreement, Messiah would establish a New Covenant. The Covenant would be based solely and strictly on God's unmerited favor! But one necessary item had to be considered. The Old Covenant's blood sacrifice didn't fit the New Covenant. God's Grace was valid only through His Chosen Messiah's blood sacrifice! Even in the Old Covenant, God had selected the scapegoat. His Messiah had become the New Covenant's scapegoat! Notice the Old Covenant provision for sin atonement by God's Law.

> *"Then Aaron shall lay both of his hands on the head of the live goat, and confess over it all the iniquities of the sons of Israel, and all their transgressions in regard to all their sins; and he shall lay them on the head of the goat and send it away into the wilderness by the hand of a man who stands in readiness. And the goat shall bear on itself all their iniquities to a solitary land; and he shall release the goat into the wilderness"*
> *(Leviticus 16:21, 22).*

The above was the true picture portrayed by the crucifixion. The Messiah Savior was our "live" sin bearer for Grace Atonement. Not just for Israel's sins but for all mankind. The Old Covenant had two "animals" involved with the Blood Atonement. The one was killed and its blood used for cleansing. It was also sprinkled on the mercy seat and in front of it. The other animal carried all their sins away. That process had to be repeated yearly by Israel. Why? Because that fulfilled the Old Covenant requirement.

God's New Covenant Atonement was not yearly but eternal! The "Son of Man" was God's Grace atonement sacrifice! It was accomplished by Jesus' divinely planned crucifixion! God's only acceptable sacrifice was "Perfect Man" and "Perfect God." The Only One who was sinless and blameless before God. He made the Old Covenant obsolete and utterly useless! God's Son had fulfilled the divinely required pre-glory activity.

Looking back at His life, mankind may discount His sacrifice. They had heard of "glory" always involved with the long life. They hadn't seen "glory" in innocent human suffering and agony! The Messiah didn't have a long life. He had lived a mere thirty-three years! Less than half a life-time, some have said. But mankind had never known such a One as Messiah! He had faced His life-time of voluntary "Son" obedience! He had spent His short life to lift "fallen" mankind! He had known, for three years at least, His Mission objective. He would have desired no other goal for His life.

He knew, early at His baptism, what the crucifixion denoted. It was His only "doorway" to reassumed majesty and glory! His Father had promised that it was readied for Him. We hastily agreed with His freedom in choosing to die. That freedom to choose was granted to every human alive. What if He had "chosen" not to die? But He did! Why? Because He had come to fulfill God's plan for mankind. He knew mankind was cursed long before His coming to earth. He had come singularly to remove that curse. He had known His divine duty. He knew He had to face the "preliminaries" to glory. Mankind's curse was removable only through His planned crucifixion.

He had informed His disciples of their abandonment and scattering. That had been fact and not guesswork. After informing them, He communicated directly with His Heavenly Father. He had that final crisis in His short life! He had to face it alone! No disciples or friends! Only His Father!

"These things Jesus spoke; and lifting up His eyes
to heaven, He said, "Father, the hour has come;

*glorify Thy Son, that the Son may glorify Thee, even
as Thou gavest Him authority over all mankind, that
to all whom Thou hast given Him, He may give eternal life. And this is eternal life, that they may know
Thee, the only true God, and Jesus Christ whom
Thou hast sent. I glorified Thee on earth, having
accomplished the work which Thou hast given Me
to do. And now, glorify Thou Me together with
Thyself, Father, with the glory which I had with
Thee before the world was" (John 17:1-5).*

We had heard Him say that He was "troubled." But that
was before the crucifixion, His prelude to Glory! We knew
it wasn't merely that He faced agony! What had really
caused Him to feel "troubled?" He hadn't feared man or
beast. How would anyone feel to have a whole life's work
forgotten? His three years' teachings totally ignored!
Attempts made to stone Him for always being truthful! Who
had a record of all those He had healed? Even His disciples,
to the very end, had needed more understanding. He knew
His "sacrifice" provided victory over sin, unbelief, and
death. He Father's acceptance was all He needed to fortify
Him. He had that absolute certainty for fulfillment and
divine spiritual peace.

We dare not consider His life with the "if" factor. His
whole life had been built on the "since" factor! His
Heavenly Father never considered, "if" His Son would
obey. He knew His Son would obey Him in everything!
How certain was His Father? "Since" His Son chose to
come to earth do die. "Since" His Son had accepted "all
authority" to complete everything. "Since" His Son
believed the Father would restore all His former Glory!

Yes, He seemed too young to die as a human, He was only
thirty-three! Was that not the bloom of maturity? Does one

count years when fulfilling God's purposes? When considering eternity, thirty-three years was so very small. Remember, He had just "put on" humanity when stepping from eternity! He was the pre-eminent Christ! His "put on" flesh was merely temporary to show God's attributes to mankind.

Recall when He first realized He must face the cross. The average man wouldn't have accepted that inevitable fate. His response would have been to avoid it and escape. But Jesus was not average man. He also was mankind's "only" escape from sin's inescapable penalty. What average man would have accepted mankind's obvious rebellion against God? Yes, that's right! Mankind had consistently disobeyed God's Laws and morally social guidelines. His Son had been a good communicator with His Father. Always, when He confronted a crisis, He consulted the Father. He had requested "strength" when He faced that "final" Crisis. His death ended a life filled with positive prayer power!

His life had continued toward that final phase of His "Glory." His whole life was lived in an "attitude" of prayer. He didn't actually have to pray before His teachings. He didn't have to pray before performing miracles, except one. Why that one time? So that God would receive full glory as His Father. Hear the words of Jesus' prayer before He had raised Lazarus.

"And so they removed the stone. And Jesus raised His eyes and said, "Father, I thank Thee that Thou heardest Me. And I knew that Thou hearest Me always; but because of the people standing around I said it, that they may believe that Thou didst send Me" (John 11:41, 42).

Everything in His life was partly related to His Glory. The good that He did was connected to His Mission. The hateful actions done against Him were "allowed" by God.

Yes, even Judas' betrayal or deception was associated with His "glory." Otherwise, the plot for crucifixion would not have been ignited. Jesus had known that His death was certain and providential. Nothing ever happened "accidentally" in His life's Mission. That Glory foundation for redemption was laid before He came to earth! He had to continue, even to die, to please the Father.

Jesus could have warned the disciples about Judas' impending betrayal. But that would have been totally unnecessary. That was not their problem. They already had more problems than they could handle. "If" the disciples had known, would they have stopped Judas? Wait! Remember what we said earlier? There were no "if" factors in Jesus' life. The disciples had never been aware of the betrayal. They had never been aware of the Pharisees' plot against Jesus. Judas' betrayal was Jesus' signal of His impending "Glory!" He had known before the Feast of the Passover. Hear His words at the Supper, as He speaks to Judas.

"And after the morsel, Satan then entered into him. Jesus therefore said to him, "What you do, do quickly." Now no one of those reclining at the table knew for what purpose He had said this to him" (John 13:27, 28).

Here we have proof that the disciples lacked adequate spiritual understanding. He expected Judas' actions to "help" to complete His Mission. The disciples did not understand until after He had died.

He proceeded to issue that other statement about His "glory." It was spoken directly to His disciples with "glowing" words. That was immediately after Judas left.

"When therefore he had gone out, Jesus said, "Now is the Son of Man glorified, and God is glorified in Him" (John 13:31).

145

What else had Jesus' death established? What about God's desire for fellowship with mankind? Had He not made man in His likeness and image? Man had broken fellowship with God by his sinful disobedience. Even after God had provided mankind with His best! Man had made many feeble attempts to regain that fellowship. Alas, man's attempts were inadequate from the beginning. He had no way to please the Creator-God! God had to take the initiative to restore His fellowship. Therefore, that was half of the God-Man's Mission! Jesus was the only divinely available solution that God would accept. His Son, the ONLY sin sacrifice, would make His fellowship eternal. If they refused His Son, the fellowship would remain broken.

True fellowship with God was rather an exclusive condition with mankind. He had His fellowship only with faith believers. His Son was the "conditional" channel. That was proclaimed to us by His Son!

"No one can come to Me, unless the Father who sent Me draws him; and I will raise him up on the last day" (John 6:44).

The Son was the only personality who had God's unbroken fellowship. Why? Because He was One with the Father! Judas had chosen to spurn the Father's fellowship. To voluntarily withdraw from His fellowship invites dangerous consequences. That always indicates opposition and disobedience to the Son and the Father!

Jesus always departed from any place He was unwelcome. He never forced Himself on any person or group. We discovered that Judas chose to leave Jesus' fellowship group. Jesus gave Judas what he wanted. Therefore, He withdrew fellowship from Judas. Judas had withdrawn himself from God's eternal Fellowship "welcome mat!"

Was it not night when Judas chose to forsake Jesus? He had chosen the working time of evildoers. He had also rejected the "Light" of God's Truth and Mercy! He had stepped into darkness to join hands with Satan. He had also chosen to step into eternity's darkness. Was he ever released from that darkness? Was he ever able to renew fellowship with God? When anyone, living on earth, rejects God's Son, there's no other way out of spiritual darkness!

"And Jesus cried and said, "He who believes in Me does not believe in Me, but in Him who sent Me. And He who beholds Me beholds the One who sent Me. I have come as light into the world, that everyone who believes in Me may not remain in darkness" (John 12:44-46).

His "Hour of Glory" introduced a new covenant and commandment. His glory activated the new commandment which proved the covenant's purpose. That showed what His motivation was for suffering and death. The capstone for His perfect love was His glory. The "final" moment for His Glory had arrived. He knew, within His being, that nothing was left undone. He had fully completed His earthly Mission for His Father! It was time for heaven's response! Was that not His Greatest Hour on earth?

We had left His tortured, limp body, hanging on the crossbeam. He had paid the full price for mankind's redemption. His Father had provided reserve strength for those final hours. That had been done to complete the "eternal life" provision. We take space here to provide proof for the religious skeptics and the unlearned. Proof of what? That His Father "spared Him" for that crucifixion ordeal. There are five recorded instances for our proof! First, Luke is very graphic in his description of one event.

147

"And all in the synagogue were filled with rage as they heard these things; and they rose up and cast Him out of the city, and led Him to the brow of the hill on which their city had been built, in order to throw Him down the cliff. But passing through their midst, He went His way" (Luke 4:28-30).

The Jews simply wanted to throw Him off the cliff! Many average Christians today did not know about that event.

The majority of proof for "sparing Him" is recorded by John. It seemed evident he loved Jesus the most. He appeared as the greatest witness of Jesus' ebbing life! Let's notice his recorded incidents where God "spared" His Son for the Crucifixion!

"They were seeking therefore to seize Him; and no man laid his hand on Him, because His hour had not yet come" (John 7:30).

"Therefore they picked up stones to throw at Him; but Jesus hid Himself, and went out of the temple" (John 8:59).

"The Jews took up stones again to stone Him" (John 10:31).

"Therefore they were seeking again to seize Him, and He eluded their grasp" (John 10:39).

The Jews persistent efforts did not disrupt God's divine plan. He had "spared" His Son to complete that Eternal Salvation Plan!

The final revelation of God to mankind had been concluded. There was no greater example of total devotion and trust. He had expected the Father's total support of His Mission. What more was expected between Holy God and Holy Son?

Even as the Father had "spared" Him, He had protected His disciples. A good teacher always watched over his learning disciples. Jesus was the "Greatest Teacher" to His disciples. The disciples belonged to God and His Son, their Messiah-Teacher. Jesus had guarded His disciples. That's what He said in His pre-arrest prayer with the Father. His disciples were still safe.

"While I was with them, I was keeping them in Thy name which Thou hast given Me; and I guarded them, and not one of them perished but the son of perdition, that the Scripture might be fulfilled" (John 17:12).

He was always aware of reclaiming His pre-existent glory! That glory will manifest divine limitless attributes. He had voluntarily laid those aside before "becoming flesh." Later, His disciples witnessed those divine and limitless attributes. We had to agree that He deserved to reclaim His "glory." He had faithfully and loyally faced His destiny here on earth. His enemies classified Him as a criminal and religious failure.

He was a special class or martyr! Why? Because He was not forgotten, as were many others. His Cross, only, brought Him "glory" and spiritual victory! How? He had achieved victory for full atonement of mankind's sins. He had achieved victory by securing God's Eternal Redemption Plan! He had achieved victory by successfully revealing God to mankind!

The Jews could not worship a non-national, personal God. They had a history of knowing "about" their Creator-God. They had plenty of traditional oral knowledge. Therefore, some weren't sure of God. Many believed only in what was seen. That belief, had caused them to become idol worshippers. But God had determined that must stop. That's why His Son came to earth. His presence provided them with personal knowledge "of" God.

The Messiah's coming allowed mankind to have divine faith contact. How? By life's highest spiritual experience providing access to our Creator. Every new believer increases glory to God through His Messiah! Only His Son can adequately present us to His Father. Man had nothing of his own with which to glorify God. It must be provided for him by God's Son.

> "I do not receive glory from men; but I know you, that you do not have the love of God in yourselves. I have come in My Father's name, and you do not receive Me; if another shall come in his own name, you will receive him. How can you believe, when you receive glory from one another, and you do not seek the glory that is from the one and only God?" (John 5:41-44).

The divine requirements for His "Hour of Glory" were finished. But His "Glory" from the Father had to affect mankind. Even after His death, He had to provide knowledge of God. It had to start on a personal basis then proceed orally. The next "hour" portrays God's Son spreading knowledge after His death! Sound impossible? Not for the God who has always done the impossible!

THE
HOUR
OF
RESURRECTION

Hour of Glory
Hour of Suffering
Hour of Revealing
Hour of Worship
Hour of Miracles
Hour of Mystery
Hour of Growth
Hour of Life

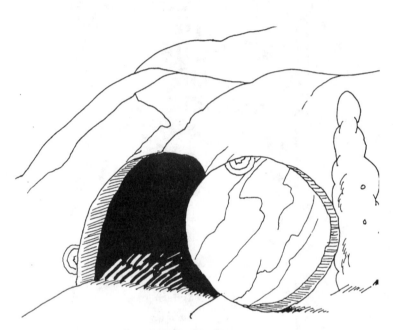

THE VICTORIOUS ESCAPE

Chapter Nine

THE HOUR OF RESURRECTION

We must start this important "hour" with a dead man. Yes! That's what I said. The man was Jesus' friend and brother of two sisters. His name was Lazarus. The story is of vital importance here. Why? To show that every truth that Jesus spoke didn't stand alone.

Jesus had just spoken to His disciples. He told them that He planned to return to Judea. The disciples heard that the Jews would try to stone Him. Lazarus' sisters came and told Jesus their brother was sick. He stayed two days longer with His disciples. Afterward, He told them that Lazarus had fallen asleep. They misunderstood what Jesus had said.

"Then Jesus therefore said to them plainly, "Lazarus is dead, and I am glad for your sakes that I was not there, so that you may believe; but let us go to him" (John 11:14, 15).

When Jesus arrived at Bethany, Lazarus was already dead! He had been in the tomb for four days! Many of the

Jews were there with Martha and Mary. An important conversation took place between Martha and Jesus.

"Martha therefore said to Jesus, "Lord, if You had been here, my brother would not have died. Even now I know that whatever You ask of God, God will give You." Jesus said to her, "Your brother shall rise again." Martha said to Him, "I know that he shall rise again in the resurrection on the last day." Jesus said to her, "I am the resurrection and the life; he who believes in Me shall live even if he dies, and everyone who lives and believes in Me shall never die. Do you believe this?" She said to Him, "Yes, Lord; I have believed that You are the Christ, the Son of God, even He who comes into the world"
(John 11:21-27).

Martha left Jesus to tell her sister about His arrival. He was still about two miles from their home. Martha, secretly, told Mary that Jesus had arrived close by. Mary left immediately and was followed by the consoling Jews. They concluded she was going to her brother's tomb. When she saw Jesus, she fell weeping at His feet. When the Jews arrived where she was, they started weeping.

"When Jesus therefore saw her weeping, and the Jews who came with her, also weeping, He was deeply moved in spirit, and was troubled, and said, "Where have you laid him?" They said to Him, "Lord, come and see." Jesus wept. And so the Jews were saying, "Behold how He loved him!"
(John 11:33-36).

When Jesus arrived at the tomb, He gave a brief command.

"Jesus said, "Remove the stone." Martha, the sister of the deceased, said to Him, "Lord, by this

154

time there will be a stench, for he had been dead
four days" (John 11:39).

We had just become involved with events of two "hours."
The "Hour of Glory" and the "Hour of Resurrection." They
had to overlap. In fact, all of Jesus' "Hours" were that way.
We noticed these especially as they related to His Glory. His
resurrection helped to launch His "after death" glory. That
also was part of God's eternal plan!

Let's return to dead Lazarus in the tomb. Remember, Jesus
always gave the Heavenly Father His due glory! In answer
to Martha's statement about the "stench," He spoke. He was
laying the foundation truth for His coming resurrection.

"Jesus said to her, "Did I not say to you, if you
believe, you will see the glory of God?" And so they
removed the stone. And Jesus raised His eyes, and
said, "Father, I thank Thee that Thou heardest Me.
And I knew that Thou hearest Me always; but
because of the people standing around I said it, that
they may believe that Thou didst send Me." And
when He had said these things, He cried out with a
loud voice, "Lazarus, come forth" (John 11:40-43).

The power of God, at His Son's request, raised Lazarus. That
was an earlier "sign" so Jews would believe His resurrection.

His preliminary "Hour" of glory was inseparable
from His Resurrection. He had told Jews the basic truth
before His glory. He tried to "show" them His association
with their God. If they showed disbelief in God's power,
they must reject His. Hear what Jesus said about His
Father's actions.

"For the Father loves the Son, and shows Him all
things that He Himself is doing; and greater works
than these will He show Him, that you may marvel.
For just as the Father raises the dead and gives

them life, even so the Son also gives life to whom
He wishes" (John 5:20, 21).

Remember, that "life" can be either physical or spiritual.
We will cite some instances later of the Old Testament
resurrections.

On a certain Sabbath, Jesus spoke of "both" resurrections. Both are attributed to His Father's given power. We
deal first with the "spiritual" life and then the "physical."

"Truly, truly, I say to you, he who hears My word,
and believes Him who sent Me, has eternal life,
and does not come into judgment, but has passed
out of death into life" (John 5:24).

While physically alive, the "spiritually" dead receives eternal, spiritual life. That comes by faith in God and His Son.
Not either One but Both entities or personalities. Now we
hear the next one.

"Truly, truly, I say to you, an hour is coming and
now is, when the dead shall hear the voice of the
Son of God; and those who hear shall live"
(John 5:25).

On that same Sabbath, He told the Jews that He possessed
divine power. The dead, from that day forward, would hear
His voice! But do you know, the Jews had not believed
Him! By disbelieving His words, they caused Him to take
action. The opportunity came with the death of Lazarus.

There at Bethany, He had planned to prove His spoken
words. He had made a promise to the dead man's sister.
What had He told her? Was it impossible for a dead man to
come alive? They were not thinking straight when they
doubted Him. They had forgotten their own religious history. They felt that anything in the past was unimportant. But
the past set the stage for Jesus' present and future. We all
recalled the prophet Elijah, raising the widow's son. That

was recorded in I Kings 17:17-24. We dare not overlook the prophet Elisha, raising a prominent couple's son. That was recorded in II Kings 4:25-35. We mention these as evidence of God's power over death. Jesus possessed that same power to resurrect those He desired.

We all have seen dead people in their caskets. Even if you talked or hollered to them, they couldn't hear. But we know Lazarus heard Jesus' voice! Of course, Lazarus was really dead. How had Jesus persuaded the Jews to believe His claims? He told them the "hour" of resurrection was coming. Of course He was referring to two kinds of dead persons. He had no intention of raising "all" the dead Jews. He was only concerned about Lazarus who was physically dead. Again, the Jews were not aware that, though alive, they were spiritually dead. Jesus had to show them that they were!

We have to provide a definition for the word "dead." We deal with it only as we speak of humans. The rest of creation only enjoys an earthly existence. Only humans have a living soul. The life for the rest of creation ends permanently on this earth. They have no "after" life existence!

Any person without Christ as Savior was dead as an unbeliever. He had been created as a being with a "soul." As an unbeliever, he was dead to God's quickening power. Through Christ only, God's spiritual quickening energizes a believers' soul. The unbelieving "dead" are not in graves. One sees them every day as physically alive and active. Symbolically, they are spiritually classified as being without life. Jesus was talking about "soul active" life. He came to give the "soul" that needed eternal life. Christ's coming was to show mankind God's available eternal life. God had intended that from the Creation. There cannot be any doubt what Jesus said and meant.

The direct opposite of death is life. Who wants to choose death when eternal life is available? He had made that clear and understandable to Mary and Martha. Since they understood His words and meaning, can't we understand? Surely He was not speaking only for the first century people? By truly believing in the Son of God, we also receive life.

"He who believes in the Son has eternal life; but he who does not obey the Son shall not see life, but the wrath of God abides on him" (John 3:36).

Those truths were applicable to both Jews and Gentiles. God had worked with Moses to establish the historical truth for the Messiah.

"And as Moses lifted up the serpent in the wilderness, even so must the Son of Man be lifted up; that whoever believes may in Him have eternal life" (John 3:14, 15).

It was the responsibility of the Jews to share their historical truths. The Gentiles also needed to hear those truths!

This "hour" had to exist in Jesus' generation. It was destined to appear as current as His presence. He had made reference to His Father many times during His Ministry. He first mentioned the "Son of God" when speaking to Nicodemus. He had to make definite His divine relationship. Long before He had confronted Martha, those words were used. They became the heart of man's faith relationship foundation.

"He who believes in Him is not judged; he who does not believe has been judged already, because he has not believed in the name of the only begotten Son of God" (John 3:18).

So, the terms had been set for life or death! They were in accordance with the Father's plan and promise. The Jews had rejected Him as the Son of God! During this "hour" He will provide indisputable truth to them. The Jews had been classified with the spiritually dead.

Take a second look at the "spiritually" dead Jews. Their sin "deadness" had caused then to ignore the "life" source. They had chosen to separate themselves from their own Messiah. Their sensuous, idolatrous existence had blinded their understanding. He had come to earth to enable them to understand. To obtain fitness for "spiritual life" they had to be resurrected from sin. That was acquired only through truly hearing the Son's voice. To ignore hearing His voice resulted in eternal judgment. To heed His words meant accepting the Father's Spokesman! He was the ONLY WAY to escape spiritual death!

That voice of God's Son was also the Father's voice. Jesus had earlier told them there would be a resurrection. They had believed that it wouldn't happen until the last day. They didn't have spiritual understanding.

"And this is the will of Him who sent Me, that of all He has given Me I lose nothing, but raise it up on the last day. For this is the will of My Father, that everyone who beholds the Son and believes in Him, may have eternal life; and I Myself will raise him up on the last day (John 6:39, 40).

They failed to understand! He had spoken of their present and His immediate future. But when was that "hour" to begin? How could He persuade them it was already started? It had begun with His spoken words!

The Giver of Life had pronounced a divine decree. It had been stated by that One with Life in Himself! It was similar to the Medes and Persians' Law. Everyone knew that Law could not be changed or revoked. It demanded immediate enforcement by the Speaker of that decree. After

He had spoken those powerful words, they expected results. The Jews had His attention at Lazarus' tomb. They were always ready to listen but not to believe. Many had also closed tight their ears toward His words. After all, to them He was just Joseph's son. The Holy Spirit was unwilling to force them to believe. Of course, Mary and Martha had believed by faith. They believed, as the other Jews, in a "last day" resurrection. Remember His reply to Martha's statement about her brother's death?

"Jesus said to her, "Your brother shall rise again." Martha said to Him, "I know that he shall rise again in the resurrection on the last day" (John 11:23, 24).

The sisters of Lazarus and other Jews lacked something. It was always the same with God's truth. They lacked perception and understanding. That always depended upon the hearers' attitude in receiving truth. They, and the other Jews, had heard Jesus' clear command! Lazarus was alive and they all saw that resurrection "power!" They all should have believed from that day forward. But did all those present that day become believers? We are sure Mary and Martha did upon seeing Lazarus alive! How could anyone that day refuse to believe? If you had been present that day, would you have believed?

"Many therefore of the Jews, who had come to Mary and beheld what He had done, believed in Him. But some of them went away to the Pharisees, and told them the things which Jesus had done" (John 11:45, 46).

Had the Pharisees rejoiced in the report of Lazarus' resurrection? Just the contrary. They were the "religious" leaders of the Jews. The event simply increased their hatred for Jesus. They, of all Jews, knew what the prophets had revealed. They were the explainers and interpreters of God's Holy Word! It seems as though the Pharisees had forgotten Jehovah's prophecies! Notice their attitude concerning Lazarus' resurrection.

"So from that day on they planned together to kill Him" (John 11:53).

What should have been the Pharisees' response to Lazarus' resurrection? They should have rejoiced and thanked Jehovah for the miracle! They had prophetic proof of Jehovah's power over death. The most vivid was Ezekiel's vision of Dry Bones. God had told him Israel's dead would hear and live. Ezekiel, as a Jew, had believed God. Surely they had believed in their own prophets! As Ezekiel had believed, shouldn't they? Was Jesus trying to recall that prophecy to their minds? How? By raising Lazarus from the dead. Notice the prophetic words.

"Then He said to me, "Son of man, these bones are the whole house of Israel; behold, they say, 'Our bones are dried up, and our hope has perished. We are completely cut off.' Therefore prophesy, and say to them, 'Thus says the Lord God, "Behold, I will open your graves and cause you to come up out of your graves, My people; and I will bring you into the land of Israel. Then you will know that I am the Lord, when I have opened your graves and caused you to come up out of your graves, My people" (Ezekiel 37:11-13).

Jesus knew that prophecy had already been partially fulfilled.

Jesus stood, at Lazarus' resurrection, in the midst of "dead" Jews. They had flesh on their bodies but their souls were dead. He stood alone among those "dead" Jews as had Ezekiel. The Jews had believed in God's prophecy. Why not believe in the interpretation and fulfillment? Jesus had

161

shown them, literally, what God had promised spiritually. Jesus was God's "breath" and presence to grant them "life!" He was God's only giver of "breath" for "soul" resurrection. Not only to all Jews but also to all Gentiles. It was guaranteed through personal faith in God's Messiah-Savior!

God had done His part. He had fulfilled Ezekiel's prophetic vision both symbolically and literally. It would not have happened without Jesus. They had been released from their spiritual captivity by their Messiah. Many stayed in their captivity by refusing God's Son! But some had already been released from that captivity. That had happened to the Samaritan woman! It had happened to Nicodemus, the teacher, from the Pharisees! Many, through Lazarus' resurrection, knew and understood that literal fulfillment. Their ignorance was replaced with the truth and faith through God's "quickening" Agent. A Jew was actually made "alive" by God's Son. He had power to give physical life! He had proved that! He had power to give "spiritual" life to the Jews first. That was the Father's plan. There stood God's "gift" to the believers among mankind. He gave His "gift" first to the Jews. Jesus had come to grant physical and spiritual quickening. He had to prove His power first in their physical realm. God had set the physical death decree because of Adam's sin. We had inherited Adam's sinful nature.

"For as in Adam all die, so also in Christ shall all be made alive" (I Corinthians 15:22).

Since God didn't renounce physical death, His grace remained necessary. His Son was operating through His Father's grace. Jesus was mankind's only Source for that Spiritual quickening. All physical or spiritual life from God, our Creator, comes through His Son. Let's extract a few words from those He had spoken to Martha.

"Jesus said to her, "I am the resurrection and the life; he who believes in Me shall live even if he dies, and everyone who lives and believes in Me shall never die. Do you believe this?"
(John 11:25, 26).

Undoubtedly, her brother Lazarus, Jesus' friend had accepted Jesus as Messiah. We had definite testimony that Lazarus was dead! God then provided testimony through His Son that Lazarus came alive! Heaven and earth's witness of Lazarus' death and resurrection cannot be refuted! Even the writer of Hebrews emphasized God's decree of death.

"And inasmuch as it is appointed for men to die once and after that the judgment, so Christ also, having been offered once to bear the sins of many, shall appear a second time for salvation without reference to sin, to those who eagerly await Him"
(Hebrews 9:27, 28).

Lazarus appeared to his sisters, fully alive, after his resurrection. Other Jews had also seen Lazarus fully resurrected!

God had appointed the proper "hour" for all to live. But one had to be "spiritually" quickened while physically alive. That had to happen before his "appointed" physical death hour. Resurrection hope was forfeited, if not quickened while physically alive. He had to first let God's Son "awaken" him spiritually. To resurrect Lazarus literally, proved that He possessed spiritual "quickening." God's Son never considered raising an unbeliever who was "spiritually" dead. There was no hope for unbelievers after their physical death.

God had granted Elijah and Elisha use of "resurrection" power. Those prophets had, with God's permission, raised two dead sons. When awakened, they were instantly alive and physically okay. They had to both be believers in God. Why? Unbelievers of God possess a hearing obstruction.

They have "spiritually" impaired hearing. In God's "spiritual" sleep only His voice will be heard. The Speaker's voice and character are easily recognized by believers. They KNOW His voice!

> *"My sheep hear My voice, and I know them, and they follow Me; and I give eternal life to them, and they shall never perish; and no one shall snatch them out of My hand" (John 10:27, 28).*

The Jews had heard Moses' words read and accepted his character. But Moses was dead and didn't know about their souls. Jesus alone knew their attitudes and their souls' spiritual condition. Had God provided Moses any power to resurrect the dead? There is no Scriptural proof. Had not God blessed the Jews during Moses' wilderness leadership?

The Son of God had just performed an epochal miracle! Even Moses' miracles can't be parallel with those performed by Jesus! That unique resurrection miracle affected all mankind's eternal destiny. He had turned water into wine. That was unusual but didn't affect all mankind. He had greatly impressed His disciples and received their praise! That miracle on Lazarus was most distinctive! He didn't just heal a sickness! He didn't just correct a physical defect! He didn't just replace a physical deficiency! He raised a Jew from the tomb! That Jew had been dead for four days. It had never been duplicated in all of history. His apostles and prophets lacked that innate power. That was Jesus' distinctive and very personal miracle! Only He had the divine power to "awaken" one's soul and body.

There were many skeptics in Jesus' miracles, and that is so today. But there are those who can easily silence the skeptics. How? By sharing a literal personal experience that proved Jesus' power. Our faith experience proved Jesus' power and silences the skeptics.

Shortly after His teaching about the two resurrections in John 5:28, 29, He met a challenge. In the city of Nain, a young man was being carried in a coffin. He was the only son of a widowed mother. A large crowd from the city was with her. What Jesus did then simply increased the Pharisees hatred toward Him.

"And when the Lord saw her, He felt compassion for her, and said to her, "Do not weep." And He came up and touched the coffin; and the bearers came to a halt. And He said, "Young man, I say to you, arise!" And the dead man sat up, and began to speak. And Jesus gave him back to his mother" (Luke 7:13-15).

Jesus spoke to the widow's dead son and he lived! The widow was glad Jesus had power to give life. The Son of God had given life to her only son. Remember this statement later. How many in that multitude knew her son was dead? Jesus' disciples had also seen the coffin. Was not a coffin used only for physically dead people? How many in that multitude saw her son sit up and speak? What did the disciples think about that miracle? Everything they saw was either real or a dream. What do you think? No! What do you believe?

In the country of the Gerasenes, Jesus was confronted by a synagogue official. He told Jesus his twelve-year-old daughter was dying. But, because of the multitude's needs, Jesus was delayed. While He was healing a serious illness, He heard a voice. Someone from the synagogue official's house had some bad news. Jesus healed the woman while hearing the bad news.

"While He was still speaking, someone came from the house of the synagogue official, saying, "Your daughter has died; do not trouble the Teacher anymore." But when Jesus heard this, He answered

him, "Do not be afraid any longer; only believe,
and she shall be made well" (Luke 8:49, 50).

Without further comment, Jesus proceeded to the synagogue official's home. He went in with only three disciples.
They were Peter, John, and James. He was alone with the
dead girl, her parents, and the disciples.

"Now they were all weeping and lamenting for
her; but He said, "Stop weeping, for she has not
died, but is asleep." And they began laughing at
Him, knowing that she had died. He, however, took
her by the hand and called, saying, "Child, arise!"
And her spirit returned, and she rose immediately;
and He gave orders for something to be given her
to eat. And her parents were amazed; but He
instructed them to tell no one what had happened"
(Luke 8:52-56).

That was proof He wasn't trying to please the skeptics.
Those three disciples had become the "inner circle" of His
Transfiguration!

He had power to raise those who were literally dead. His
resurrection "hour" came on time. Ask Jairus and his wife.
They will tell you the truth about their precious daughter. Ask
the widow of Nain. She will tell you the truth about her only
son. Also, ask Mary and Martha about Lazarus. They will tell
you their brother was raised from the dead. How are we sure
that those three events had happened? God's Son had hun-
dreds of witnesses plus the resurrected persons!

God's Son possessed power over life and death. His
voice spoke healing to the deaf, blind, and crippled. His
voice had penetrated the realm of death and restored life!
His voice injected life into any believer's soul! No grave
was beyond the sound of His voice. No believer was overlooked or forgotten by Him. He entered the "resurrection"

hour to assure power for raising everyone. That was part of His Messianic Commission. His earthly responsibility to His Father was finished after the resurrection.

The Father had set the exact time for His Son's Crucifixion. He also set the exact time for His Son's resurrection. In God's time realm, we find nothing left to chance! Since those times had been divinely set, nothing could change them!

His resurrection had been enacted according to schedule. We knew He was dead! We knew He had been buried in Joseph of Arimathea's tomb. Also, we knew their Law insisted on a definite burial time. Jesus had been classified as a criminal by the Jews. They claimed He had committed a sin worthy of crucifixion. He was regarded as a normal, law-breaking human being.

"And if a man has committed a sin worthy of death, and he is put to death, and you hang him on a tree, his corpse shall not hang all night on a tree, but you shall surely bury him on the same day (for he who is hanged is accused of God), so that you do not defile your land which the Lord your God gives you as an inheritance" (Deuteronomy 21:22, 23).

Since the Jews counted Him as an ordinary man, He must hang. He was not exempted from Pilate's pressured decision. The Jewish people dared not defy their own Law penalty. Their Pharisees had known all about the Law. It had been observed by Jews for many centuries. The person Jesus, they thought, was just another human cursed by God. All they saw was Jesus' humanity as ugly as theirs. Their own sin corrupted their eyes from seeing Jesus' divinity! Paul the Apostle later saw the prophetic portrayal of Deuteronomy 21:22, 23. He saw the truth only through his spiritual faith sight. He showed us how God's Grace, through Jesus, erased our sin curse!

167

"Christ redeemed us from the curse of the Law, having become a curse for us – for it is written, "CURSED IS EVERYONE WHO HANGS ON A TREE" – in order that in Christ Jesus the blessing of Abraham might come to the Gentiles, so that we might receive the promise of the Spirit through faith" (Galatians 3:13, 14).

The One who provided "spiritual" resurrection for mankind is dead. Was that "spiritual" resurrection ever recalled by His Father? He had spoken of "dual" resurrections! While alive, He was able to guarantee continued spiritual resurrection! While alive He was able to guarantee hope of physical resurrection! No one else had the power to resurrect the physically dead. No one else had the power to resurrect the believing soul.

How would the people remember the Son's words about resurrections? How could He prove His words were the truth? Maybe if He were resurrected from the dead! Who could have accomplished that? Not His disciples! They had doubts about His teachings! Not the Pharisees! They even twisted the Law to please themselves! But wait! Had we already forgotten His earlier claim? Had He not said those powerful words in John 10:18? He had authority to lay down His life. Nobody forced Him to die. He had authority to take up His life again. Nobody had power or ability, on earth, to resurrect anybody. Jesus alone received that commandment from His heavenly Father.

When He was alive, the crowds recognized His healing power. His true disciples recognized His healing power. On the other hand, the Pharisees disclaimed His divine ability to change lives. Yet, we have proof He possessed all divinely granted power.

*"And all the multitudes were trying to touch Him,
for power was coming from Him and healing them
all" (Luke 6:19).*

Since He had divine power granted Him, what about self-resurrection? It was humanly impossible but not divinely impossible!

Jesus came to be identified as the Giver of Life! Death had already been mandated by God in the beginning. Since it was initiated by God because of sin, God alone must override it. That's what He sent Jesus to do. He alone had established eternal life for all souls. Of course, eternal life for believers or unbelievers involves a resurrection. His "life" offer was received instantly and retained forever! Before His Incarnation, mankind had no way of escaping "soul" death. Those who refused Him, by faith, are resurrected to eternal condemnation. That is the spiritual death sentence. To have refused Him by faith also refused His resurrection ability. Since the body was already buried, the soul was withheld that resurrection joy!

Messiah's resurrection category was determined while He was physically alive. So are mankind's resurrection status decided while he's physically alive. Before His Crucifixion, Messiah knew He would be resurrected. God had sealed that decision through His Son's obedient Incarnation. Therefore, mankind's "souls" resurrections are sealed through Messiah's resurrection. All mankind's resurrection hopes are based upon faith in God's Messiah!

Notice the victorious event that guaranteed His promise to mankind. There was no voice outside His tomb to resurrect Him. He alone had resurrection power! Was there a tomb adequate to imprison God's Only Son? Since Jesus had the resurrection Key, His power opened the tomb from "inside!" He had to fulfill His promises made to mankind!

169

He never made a promise He was unable to keep! The Son was like His Father who also kept promises.

Have you heard this statement made by anyone? I saw it, but I don't understand it. On the first day of the week, Mary Magdalene came to the tomb. She saw the tomb's great sealed stone already rolled away. We are amazed how unbelief always assumes the wrong conclusion. Mary ran and told two disciples what she had concluded.

"And so she ran and came to Simon Peter, and the other disciple whom Jesus loved, and said to them, "They have taken away the Lord out of the tomb, and we don't know where they have laid Him"
(John 20:2).

Peter and John ran to the tomb to see for themselves. John arrived first, looked in, but did not enter. Peter arrived and entered the tomb. Then John entered the tomb, and what he saw caused him to believe. He saw no body but knew Jesus had been resurrected. All the disciples didn't have the faith of John.

"For as yet they did not understand the Scripture, that He must rise again from the dead. So the disciples went away again to their homes"
(John 20:9, 10).

The disciples had forgotten Jesus' teachings after cleansing the temple. He knew the Pharisees and other Jews didn't understand. He expected His disciples to have understanding.

"Jesus answered and said to them, "Destroy this temple, and in three days I will raise it up." The Jews therefore said, "It took forty-six years to build this temple, and will You raise it up in three days?" But He was speaking of the temple of His body. When therefore He was raised from the dead,

His disciples remembered that He said this; and they believed the Scripture, and the word which Jesus had spoken" (John 2:19-22).

Even though the disciples lacked understanding, two women were hopeful. Notice their response at the tomb experience.

"And looking up, they saw that the stone had been rolled away, although it was extremely large. And entering the tomb, they saw a young man sitting at the right, wearing a white robe; and they were amazed. And he said to them, "Do not be amazed; you are looking for Jesus the Nazarene, who has been crucified. He has risen; He is not here; behold, here is the place where they laid Him. But go, tell His disciples and Peter, 'He is going before you into Galilee; there you will see Him, just as He said to you.'" And they went out and fled from the tomb, for trembling and astonishment had gripped them; and they said nothing to anyone, for they were afraid" *(Mark 16:4-8).*

Who were those men in white robes? They were God's angelic messengers who had very important news! It was specifically for His Son's disciples and all Jews. God still wanted the Jewish people to believe His Son! He had provided all necessary proof for His divine purpose. His Son had overcome death and escaped the tomb! God's angelic messengers had verified His Only Son's heavenly victory! Jesus' disciples had every reason to proclaim heaven's powerful proof! How much longer must mankind wait to believe those truths?

We also had the unusual experience of two unnamed believers. They were traveling to Emmaus from

Jerusalem. The two were talking about Jesus' crucifixion, death, and burial.

"And they were conversing with each other about all these things which had taken place. And it came about while they were conversing and discussing, Jesus Himself approached and began traveling with them. But their eyes were prevented from recognizing Him. And they approached the village where they were going, and He acted as though He would go farther. And they urged Him, saying, "Stay with us, for it is getting toward evening, and the day is now nearly over." And He went in to stay with them. And it came about when He had reclined at the table with them, He took the bread and blessed it, and breaking it, He began giving it to them. And their eyes were opened and they recognized Him; and He vanished from their sight" (Luke 24:14-16; 28-31).

The Resurrected Messiah proceeded to make several more appearances. He next appeared to the ten disciples with Thomas absent. After another eight days He appeared to the eleven disciples with Thomas present. He appeared, over a period of forty days, teaching about God's Kingdom. Paul, the Apostle, said Jesus appeared to more than five hundred believers. The Scriptures prove He made twelve post-resurrection appearances. How can mankind refute those truths? They had tried two different approaches.

First, don't provide all the necessary information about the event. Individuals didn't believe in the "impossible" works God used in fulfillment! Notice the response of the disciples to the two women's words. Their information wasn't complete for the disciples.

"And these words appeared to them as nonsense, and they would not believe them" (Luke 24:11).

The women had just shared what the disciples had considered "impossible." Mankind can't believe what they deem impossible. Many individuals found it difficult to believe God's displayed truth. Yes, the disciples, and other Jews, couldn't accept God's "impossible" results! There are people like that in every generation of mankind.

Second, provide an outright lie and fortify it with bribery. Of course that was easy when approaching the Jews. They didn't accept Jesus as the Jewish Messiah. In no way was He accepted or recognized as their Savior. They didn't acknowledge Him when He was alive nor would they accept Him as being resurrected! The religious leaders had no trouble bribing someone to betray Him. Their devious methods continued in their opposition of that Messiah. They continued deceiving people concerning Jesus' proven resurrection. Notice their actions during Jesus' early post-resurrection appearance.

> *"Then Jesus said to them, "Do not be afraid; go and take word to My brethren to leave for Galilee, and there they shall see Me." Now while they were on their way, behold, some of the guard came into the city and reported to the chief priests all that had happened. And when they had assembled with the elders and counseled together, they gave a large sum of money to the soldiers, and said, "You are to say, 'His disciples came by night and stole Him away while we were asleep.' And if this should come to the governor's ears, we will win him over and keep you out of trouble." And they took the money and did as they had been instructed; and this story was widely spread among the Jews, and is to this day" (Matthew 28:10-15).*

Was that a prime example of corrupt religious leaders? They lied to religious people while they manipulated and appeased others.

A brief word must be said about God's sovereignty. God is the Creator and Ruler of the universe. He consults no one in making decisions. He can "take" life from those who are physically alive! He can "give" life to those who are physically dead! The Messiah came not as Spirit but "put on flesh and dwelt among us." He came to look, live, love, and die as a human. He had to appear in human form for mankind's benefit. That was the only way to fulfill our resurrection to life! That resurrection to eternal life was sealed only for true believers. Jesus activated God's judgment and spiritual death for all unbelievers.

By faith He calls all mankind to hear and believe. He became your Personal Savior or your divine Judge. You alone are given the choice for personal eternal destiny. In the final resurrection, His Voice will determine your eternal abode. Unbelievers will confront God as their Judge for eternal condemnation! Believers will confront God with Jesus as their Grace Defender! Jesus will only speak for His believers. He had decided that all who heard His voice will live. All who ignored His voice, having no saving faith, would stay judged.

In the final analysis, we have some irrefutable resurrection witnesses. The account was given to us by Luke. He was also credited with writing the record in Acts. We refer to his words after hearing the Emmaus men's account. An incident that took place while they were relating their experiences to the Risen Jesus.

"And while they were telling these things, He Himself stood in their midst. But they were startled and frightened and thought that they were seeing a

spirit. And He said to them, "Why are you trou-
bled, and why do doubts arise in your hearts? See
My hands and My feet, that it is I Myself; touch Me
and see, for a spirit does not have flesh and bones
as you see that I have" (Luke 24:36-40).

He had appeared twice to His disciples to prove His Resurrection. He presented to those He trained that final proof appearance. They were His most fruitful witnesses!

"To these He also presented Himself alive, after
His suffering, by many convincing proofs, appear-
ing to them over a period of forty days, and
speaking of the things concerning the kingdom of
God" (Acts 1:3).

God had provided a divine witness for Jesus' resurrection power. His Son's disciples had first, by sight, witnessed that power! Their faith then became unshakeable when they proclaimed those experiences! They suddenly acknowledged and assumed that awesome human responsibility! Peter, the weakest pre-resurrection disciple, became the fearless resurrection witness! Notice the disciples' bold witness as they spoke to the Sanhedrin. They were ordered not to teach anything in Jesus' name. Hear their forceful response!

"But Peter and the apostles answered and said,
"We must obey God rather than men. The God of
our fathers raised up Jesus, whom you had put to
death by hanging Him on a cross. He is the one
whom God exalted to His right hand as a Prince
and a Savior, to grant repentance to Israel, and
forgiveness of sins. And we are witnesses of these
things; and so is the Holy Spirit, whom God has
given to those who obey Him" (Acts 5:29-32).

The disciples, led by Peter, were fulfilling the mandate of Jesus. God never acted in history without providing reliable witnesses. His Son was the greatest "human" witness for all mankind! The Holy Spirit was the greatest "invisible" witness to mankind! Only Godly believers, by faith, experience the invisible Spirit's witness. God's "divine-human" witness will always reign in believers' lives! His "invisible" witness, the Holy Spirit, can be experienced today! Have YOU seen Him by faith? The Holy Spirit remains God's faithful witness for Heavenly Truth!

"When the Helper comes, whom I will send to you from the Father, that is the Spirit of truth, who proceeds from the Father, He will bear witness of Me, and you will bear witness also, because you have been with Me from the beginning" (John 15:26, 27).

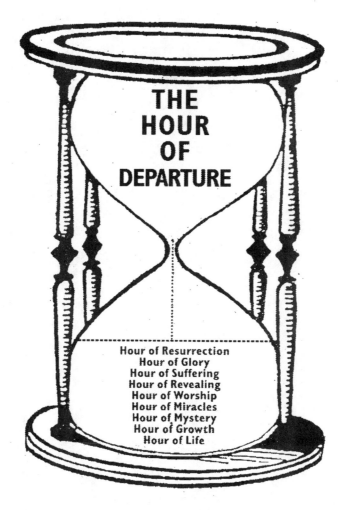

THE HOUR OF DEPARTURE

Hour of Resurrection
Hour of Glory
Hour of Suffering
Hour of Revealing
Hour of Worship
Hour of Miracles
Hour of Mystery
Hour of Growth
Hour of Life

ASCENDED INTO PARADISE

Chapter Ten

THE HOUR OF DEPARTURE

Jesus had accomplished that victory over sin, death, and eternal condemnation. He had been given all authority to keep His promise. His resurrection had been completed! There was plenty of proof available. How far ahead had He known He would depart?

"Now before the Feast of the Passover, Jesus knowing that His hour had come that He should depart out of this world to the Father, having loved His own who were in the world, He loved them to the end" (John 13:1).

Here He had mentioned an obvious and "seen" physical departure. His discipled believers would observe a literal departure event. They had not actually seen His resurrection but it happened! The resurrection involved a fully spiritual event even though unseen. Before His departure, or ascension, He must appear totally physical. His promised departure involved His invisible Heavenly Father our

179

Creator! Had we forgotten Jesus' words associating Him with total divinity? We must review them for the sake of clearer understanding.

> *"And now, glorify Thou Me together with Thyself,*
> *Father, with the glory which I had with Thee before*
> *the world was. But now I have come to Thee; and*
> *these things I speak in the world, that they may have*
> *My joy made full in themselves" (John 17:5, 13).*

Here Jesus spoke in the framework of God's eternal NOW! In that framework, everything had been accomplished! His "hour" of glory had to unite with His departure. His resurrection and departure were enacted by full power and control.

Jesus' love wasn't interrupted or changed by His final departure. His decision for leaving automatically guaranteed the Divine Family reunion. What a beautiful sight that was in Heaven! No one could imagine or portray that glorious, majestic event! But even after His departure some great truths had surfaced.

The Messiah had chosen to enter the realm of earth. The Father had not "forced" His Son to come. His Son had voluntarily chosen to depart from Heaven. Nothing was done without targeting God's divine plan for mankind. He had that departure plan always ready to be activated. He was not driven out by the Jewish priests. The power of Satan didn't influence His departure! No power on earth caused Him to shorten His Mission! His Father didn't suggest that His Son's Mission be shortened. We find no reference that the Father ordered Him back! He had satisfactorily accomplished all requirements for mankind's salvation! He couldn't have departed until those three divinely fulfilled words. "IT IS FINISHED," as found in John 19:30.

Had His departure created a sense of loss? If so, for whom? Not for the Sanhedrin, they were glad He was gone! Not for His earthly brothers, they never did understand Him! Not for unbelieving Jews, to them, their Moses was greater!

His departure had surely affected His eleven chosen disciples. We remember that Judas had hung himself because of the betrayal. The disciples had never before witnessed such love for mankind! Was that not the reason for Jesus' coming from Heaven? It was also the reason He had to depart from earth. Had He not portrayed that unforgettable example of Godly Love? He had known that His departure was inevitable. His departure had assured His unending love for the disciples. His departure and their separation provided His love's greatest test. How could the disciples, or any believer, forget those words?

In My Father's house are many dwelling places; if
it were not so, I would have told you; for I go to
prepare a place for you" (John 14:1, 2).

Doesn't that sound like words of continued love and concern?

Why should that be so hard for believers to understand? Had not our Creator-Savior prepared a world for our "earthly" existence? God had not polluted His earth with disobedience and rebellion. Mankind had made it unfit for peaceful relationships and God-centered worship! Every generation has plunged man into greater separation from God! Our Creator-Father knew that would happen, and it did! He foreknew all mankind's evil intentions and their Godless love! He provided the remedy for mankind's needed change of existence! So, Jesus departed from Heaven to guarantee our "better" world!

"He was in the world, and the world was made
through Him, and the world did not know Him. He

181

came to His own, and those who were His own did
not receive Him" (John 1:10, 11).

He stayed on earth until His divine Mission was completed. The Father knew that total mankind wouldn't recognize His Son. Those who did recognize Him, by faith, had been changed. They were then guaranteed entrance into Jesus' prepared dwelling places. All believers are classified as being "out of this world."

"They were not of the world, even as I am not of
the world" (John 17:16).

Jesus had to depart because He belonged to another world. That world remained without sin, hatred, and disobedience. Every believer is destined also to depart to His "world!"

He would depart from them physically, but they wouldn't be alone. He made another promise which was fulfilled after He departed. He had given them notice far in advance of departure.

"But I tell you the truth, it is to your advantage
that I go away; for if I do not go away, the Helper
shall not come to you; but if I go, I will send Him
to you. But when He, the Spirit of truth, comes, He
will guide you into all truth; for He will not speak
on His own initiative, but whatever He hears, He
will speak; And He will disclose to you what is to
come" (John 16:7, 13).

All of God's plan for mankind's destiny was properly coordinated. Jesus' planned and orderly departure necessitated the Holy Spirit's entrance. As He promised His disciples, so He promised all believers. The Holy Spirit keeps God's children in fellowship with Him. Jesus' departure sealed our relationship with God's Son, and Spirit. Jesus notified believers about our unique Oneness with His Father! Again, He also showed believers' spiritual relationship before His departure.

"And I am no more in the world; and yet they themselves are in the world, and I come to Thee, Holy Father, keep them in Thy name, the name which Thou hast given Me, that they may be one, even as We are" (John 17:11).

We remembered those initial words before mentioning the coming Helper. He had to prepare them gradually for His post-resurrection departure.

"But now I am going to Him who sent Me; and none of you asks Me, 'Where are You going?'" (John 16:5).

They had never expected Him to cease being their Teacher. They had never expected Him to be separated from them! They had never expected Him to be crucified and die! He had humanly, and as God's Son, prepared the disciples. The day for testing their understanding had arrived! Had their response been as mere humans to any calamity? Had Jesus become "out of sight and out of mind?" NO! The Acts account proved they never forgot their Truth commitment. There was not doubt that their Teacher's Truth still lived!

The Holy Spirit's coming had been fulfilled as Jesus promised. His initial coming was to empower the disciples for sharing. As they shared Jesus' Truth, the Holy Spirit brought conviction. Look at the strong Scriptural proof!

"And they were all filled with the Holy Spirit and began to speak with other tongues, as the Spirit was giving them utterance. Now there were Jews living in Jerusalem, devout men, from every nation under heaven" (Acts 2:4, 5).

We must not give the disciples any credit or praise. They were simply doing what they were ordered to do! They were to proclaim the truth first to the Jews. That's what their

Teacher had instructed when He trained them. Weren't they strictly following His orders?

> *"These twelve Jesus sent out after instructing them, saying, "Do not go in the way of the Gentiles, and do not enter any city of the Samaritans; but rather go to the lost sheep of the house of Israel"*
> *(Matthew 10:5, 6).*

Jesus had not changed those initial instructions before He departed. The Holy Spirit came not to change but to fulfill His truth. Had all the Jews accepted Jesus before His departure? Any student of the Scriptures knows the answer. The Book of Acts shows the Spirit's greatest conviction results. The disciples were "Spirit-filled" and that Helper brought conviction. We must give God all the glory and praise for results!

> *"And He, when He comes, will convict the world concerning sin, and righteousness, and judgment; concerning sin, because they do not believe in Me; and concerning righteousness, because I go to the Father, and you no longer behold Me; and concerning judgment, because the ruler of this world had been judged" (John 16:8-11).*

The divine signal had been given for the Holy Spirit. He had been prepared for His departure from Heaven. Jesus had to depart from earth first, according to divine plan! He had to reactivate and reassume His "spiritual" Kingdom! That was what He tried to tell Pilate before the Crucifixion.

> *"Jesus answered, "My kingdom is not of this world. If My kingdom were of this world, then My servants would be fighting, that I may not be delivered up to the Jews; but as it is, My kingdom is not of this realm" (John 18:36).*

Whenever He departed, the Jewish idea of Messiahship had to disappear. The Holy Spirit, the new invisible Teacher and Helper, had appeared.

"But the Helper, the Holy Spirit, whom the Father will send in My name, He will teach you all things, and bring to your remembrance all that I said to you" (John 14:26).

The Father's "New Teacher" was totally and fully spiritual! He is the constant reminder to mankind about Jesus' teachings.

Jesus departed as earthly Teacher to become our Heavenly mediator. The Apostle Paul wrote to Timothy about Jesus' new role. His writings placed Jesus' reason for departure in proper perspective. What he said made it so clear for us.

"This is good and acceptable in the sight of God our Savior, who desires all men to be saved and to come to the knowledge of the truth. For there is one God, and one Mediator also between God and men, the man Christ Jesus, who gave Himself as a ransom for all, the testimony borne at the proper time" (I Timothy 2:3-6).

Did not Jesus' departure portray leaving one existence for another? Wasn't that what He came to do for all mankind? What was His departure's importance as related to His Mission? He had to report the victorious results which concluded His Mission! We knew that His report contained nothing unsatisfactory or displeasing. It was divinely impossible for Him to have failed! Was He not aware of full divine power and authority? He had earlier stated His human-divine position to the Jews.

"And He who sent Me is with Me; He has not left Me alone, for I always do the things that are pleasing to Him" (John 8:29).

185

Nothing or anyone on earth had changed His timely departure!

The Father's Son experienced the transportation to a totally divine existence. His thirty-three year earthly Mission had been successfully completed. His brief "earthly tour of duty" was over. His Mission and His earthly actions complimented the Father's position. His earthly existence was unchangeable as was His unchangeable future! His temporary earthly interlude had provided mankind that eternal Heavenly existence. Without His departure, God's Creation Plan had no redemptive relationship.

We all knew His "heavenly" departure was the Incarnation. Before that departure, He had clothed His divinity with Self-limitations. He was not forced, but had willingly chosen human frailties. He had voluntarily decided to take Heaven's Light to mankind! Without His heavenly departure mankind would have remained in "spiritual" darkness!

His "earthly" departure brought guaranteed reunion with His Heavenly Father! That was completed when He separated Himself from His disciples. Not only the Jews but all mankind experienced His separation. In spite of His physical departure, His love remained on earth. It had stayed "glowing" in all true believers' hearts!

His triumphant departure could have made the disciples feel abandoned. Why? They had been living mostly by "sight" for three years. Those horrible pre-departure events had almost erased their weak faith. We knew they had abandoned Him after the crucifixion. He had spoken those words to them in John 16:32. Jesus never abandoned those He loved! There was no unfaithfulness by Jesus to anyone on earth or in heaven! Obedience and faithfulness were basic attributes connected with His Mission. His divine-human nature demanded that He excel in those attributes. He expected those attributes to exist in all true believers. The disciples' "sight" walk had ended. They must begin "walking" by their tested faith.

We mentioned earlier that He loved to be around people. Remember His experiences in Chapter Four, "The Hour of Miracles?" He loved His disciples in a double situation. His love for them as their Teacher on earth! His love for them also as their Savior!

Many months before His departure, His disciples walked with confidence! Their Teacher had worked miracles! Who would have dared to oppose their Teacher? Their security was based on their sight, not their faith. He knew their weakness of faith in His divine role! He knew their faith would fail them in those dangerous hours! Their spirituality had never faced such extreme testing! As His death, so His departure, greatly strained their immature spirituality. He knew that!

In spite of all He knew about their weakness, He still loved them. Had He not taught and trained them the Truth? In mankind's times of weakness, His Truth will provide strength! He knew their limitations because He also had "become" human. If He forsook them, it would displease His Heavenly Father. That was unthinkable!

He had chosen to provide His sacrificial purpose for them. Their guilt for forsaking Him lay heavy on their hearts. They weren't able to deal with it after His death. So, before His departure, He had to confront their guilt. If He hadn't forgiven them, their guilt would remain. Unknown to them, He had planned a "special" confrontation. They had to experience their Teacher-Savior's forgiveness before He departed. That spiritual healing, soul-cleansing experience happened in John Chapter 21.

We must insert a sad note before finishing His departure. It relates to His earthly, human efforts to spread Truth. The Scribes and Pharisees had led the Jews against Him. He had wanted the Jews to accept His divine origin. They had rejected Him and became His enemies. They had committed two personal and national sins. They had turned their backs on their Creator-God! They had also rejected Heaven's Only Sacrifice for mankind's sin!

No one had ever been able to reverse God's Laws. Only the Creator-Redeemer has power to reverse His Laws! Had He not controlled the Laws of the universe for His purpose? He could do anything for His Chosen Nation of Israel. We don't have space to mention all of them. Let us notice one that affected our earth's orbital path.

In the Book of Joshua, the Lord slew Israel's enemies at Gibeon. God had chosen to fight for Israel. Joshua was God's man and Israel's leader at that time. The word Joshua means, "YAHWEH IS SALVATION." Here was how God overrode one of His Creation Laws. God did it to fulfill His purpose for Chosen Israel. These Scriptures show God's Omnipotence!

> *"So the sun stood still, and the moon stopped, until the nation avenged themselves of their enemies. Is it not written in the book of Jashar? And the sun stopped in the middle of the sky, and did not hasten to go down for about a whole day. And there was no day like that before it or after it, when the Lord listened to the voice of a man; for the Lord fought for Israel" (Joshua 10:13, 14).*

Since God did that singular action for Israel's survival, had He forgotten them? You may ask how Joshua's account relates to our Messiah!

God's Law of gravity keeps only objects and humans earth-bound. The Law of sin keeps mankind spiritually bound on earth. Our God-Man Jesus, personally reversed the Gravity Law in His departure. Was He not the Author of that Law? He alone possessed power to spiritually reverse the sin Law. His departure provided the only hope for unbelievers. His earthly exodus provided a unique freedom for true believers. Notice the Apostle Paul's comment about that Law of sin.

> *"But the Scripture has shut up all men under sin, that the promise by faith in Jesus Christ might be given to those who believe. But before faith came, we were kept in custody under the law, being shut up to the faith which was later to be revealed. Therefore the Law has become our tutor to lead us to Christ, that we may be justified by faith"* *(Galatians 3:22-24).*

Our departure to Heaven is guaranteed through divine grace. God's spiritual drawing power was energized by His Love and Grace. That same Grace is available through faith in His Son. All that He accomplished before His departure affected all mankind. Everyone on earth needs God's Grace because all mankind sinned. We are all the progeny of Adam, the first man. We inherited the "sin" gene, or virus, through Adam's disobedience. The Apostle Paul gave us a simple but powerful statement!

> *"For as in Adam all die, so also in Christ all shall be made alive"* *(I Corinthians 15:22).*

All believers, by faith, have been promised earth to heaven departure. That applied to both Jew and Gentile believers in Christ. Jesus, after departing earth, knew where He would dwell eternally! Wherever He dwells eternally, we shall also abide there! Didn't He say, earlier, the main purpose for His departure? To prepare a dwelling place for those believing in Him!

"And the witness is this, that God has given us eternal life, and this life is in His Son. He who has the Son has the life; he who does not have the Son of God does not have the life. These things I have written to you who believe in the name of the Son of God, in order that you may know that you have eternal life" (I John 5:11-13).

Our Savior had departed to reoccupy that vacated Heavenly Glory! His full Divine Majesty was preserved and ready for Him! He had earned the full "responsibility" to mediate for believers. He had accomplished everything for mankind's earthly "spiritual" decisions.

"Every one therefore who shall confess Me before men, I will also confess him before My Father who is in heaven. But whoever shall deny Me before men, I will also deny him before My Father who is in heaven" (Matthew 10:32, 33).

Shortly after His statement of departing, He announced His earth to heaven role. He had done so, primarily for His disciples' continued understanding. (It is mentioned here to give the reader deeper understanding.) Our Master's words left no room for uncertainty or doubt. It is the greatest verse to encompass His earthly Mission.

"Jesus said to him, "I am the way, and the truth, and the life; no one comes to the Father, but through Me" (John 14:6).

He was and is the Heavenly Father's only Eternal Life Channel. How can any segment of mankind lack the necessary understanding?

In those last pre-departure moments, He concentrated on disciples' awareness. Peter had his denials forgiven and was challenged to obedience! The disciples learned that time and space cannot contain Him! They finally recognized His Divine ability to know all things! He related that last awareness to their livelihood! He had firmly and knowingly told them where to fish! He knew the place where the fish exceeded the normal size. He knew where the "large" ones were available for catching.

"Jesus said to them, "Bring some of the fish which you have now caught." Simon Peter went up, and drew the net to land, full of large fish, a hundred and fifty-three; and although there were so many, the net was not torn" (John 21:10, 11).

He then prepared the disciples for their "last" earthly fellowship experience!

He had done everything for them during those three years. Before His departure He clearly solved all their unasked questions. They knew He was their "living" former, earthly Messiah-Teacher! He was not a ghost or apparition but their MESSIAH! He had talked at length and eaten with them. He was Real! After He promised them the Holy Spirit's Power, He departed. They actually saw Him depart!

"And after He had said these things, He was lifted up while they were looking on, and a cloud received Him out of their sight. And as they were gazing intently into the sky while He was departing, behold, two men in white clothing stood beside them; and they also said, "Men of Galilee, why do you stand looking into the sky? This Jesus, who has been taken up from you into heaven, will come in just the same way as you have watched Him go into heaven" (Acts 1:9-11).

His Incarnation was the first of His "greatest" miracles. His Departure was the last "greatest" miracle. Both His first and His last were to seal mankind's destiny.

The "Hours" of His earthly existence had stopped running. His earthly time had run out! The greatest dweller among mankind had left the earthly scene! Those Greatest Hours belonged only to the Greatest "existing" Personality! The disciples continued declaring the indelible "experiences" He had provided.

Could not the Messiah's Mission be capsulated in verse? What do you think? The Apostle Paul did so in his Epistle to Timothy.

"And by common confession great is the mystery of godliness:
He was revealed in the flesh,
Was vindicated in the Spirit,
Beheld by angels,
Proclaimed among the nations,
Believed on in the world,
Taken up into glory." (I Timothy 3:16).

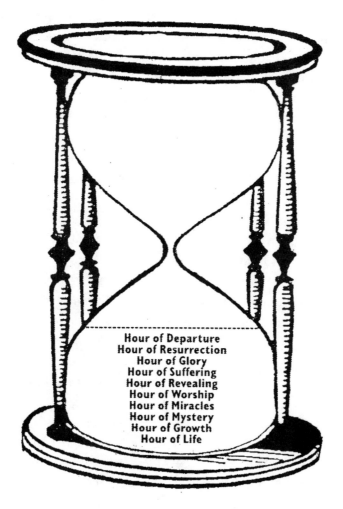

Hour of Departure
Hour of Resurrection
Hour of Glory
Hour of Suffering
Hour of Revealing
Hour of Worship
Hour of Miracles
Hour of Mystery
Hour of Growth
Hour of Life

Epilogue

HE'S GONE! They saw Him leave! But WAIT! Haven't we overlooked His greatest promise to all His believers??? The eleven disciples immediately returned to Jerusalem's upper room. They had an important task or problem to pray about. They had to ask God's choice in selecting another disciple. And they did, under God's guidance.

But what was that statement made by the two men in white? Of course! He was just reminding them of their Messiah's Great Promise.

"And if I go and prepare a place for you, I will
come again, and receive you to Myself; that where
I am, there you may be also" (John 14:3).

Yes, that's it! He's going to come again! He always kept His promises! The Apostle Paul believed that and told the Thessalonian believers.

"For the Lord Himself will descend from heaven
with a shout, with the voice of the archangel, and
with the trumpet of God; and the dead in Christ
shall rise first. Then we who are alive and remain
shall be caught up together with them in the clouds
to meet the Lord in the air, and thus we shall always
be with the Lord" (I Thessalonians 4:16, 17).

Our Heavenly Father had already guaranteed that triumphant return! "JAH" which means, "HALLELUJAH." He is EL SHADDAI! EL ELYON! JEHOVAH! YAHWEH! The ALPHA and OMEGA! HALLELUJAH!

"Life's Hourglass"

Most people watch the Hourglass
As sand flows from the top;
They see that sand begin its flow
But cannot make it stop.

It passes through the tiny hole
But always grain by grain;
Yet neither hurries not slows its flow,
Unlike the falling rain.

We are in God's Hourglass of Life,
And live each passing day;
We have no power to stop its flow
Or speed it on its way.

Observe the sand, as grain by grain,
Each finds its proper place;
God has His plan for every life,
For all the human race.

Unlike the sand we live and breathe,
As through His strength we strive;
To touch a life with love and joy,
And keep one's hope alive.

As we move through life's Hourglass,
We follow first then lead;
And take our place as others have,
In helping those in need.

You are a special grain of life
Who moves with unsung fame;
To bring that hope to other hearts
Because you know God's name.